HOW TO TAKE & DEVELOP BLACK & WHITE PHOTOGRAPHS

To Melissa
with love —
I'm very, very proud
of you.
Ellie

HOW TO TAKE & DEVELOP

BLACK & WHITE PHOTOGRAPHS

MICHAEL FREEMAN

NEW BURLINGTON BOOKS

A QUINTET BOOK

Published by New Burlington Books
6 Blundell Street
London N7 9BH

ISBN 1-85348-957-3

Reprinted 1995

This book was designed and produced by
Quintet Publishing Limited
6 Blundell Street
London N7 9BH

Art Director: Peter Bridgewater
Design Director: Ian Hunt
Designer: Jonathan Roberts
Editors: Christopher Dickie, Shaun Barrington
Photographer: Michael Freeman

Typeset in Great Britain by
Central Southern Typesetters, Eastbourne
Manufactured in Hong Kong by
Regent Publishing Services Limited
Printed in Singapore by
Star Standard Industries (Pte) Ltd

CONTENTS

MAIN MOM
TALK

More than ever before, black-and-white film is the medium of personal expression in photography. Colour may dominate the market because of its realism, but the results in black-and-white can be controlled much more closely, and more easily. Its simplicity comes from recording everything on a single scale of tones. The refinement of a monochrome image lies in the way it forces both the photographer and the viewer of the final print to see objects and scenes more graphically – as made up of shapes, lines and tonal differences.

Nothing could be simpler than modern black-and-white film and print handling. For decades, photography depended on this chemistry, and the formation of an image in silver remains the first step in every kind of film, including all the colour emulsions. Light-sensitive crystals of silver halide in a single layer react when the camera's shutter is opened, and a single solution of developer converts them to silver metal. There is nothing more complicated to it than this, and the tolerances of exposure and processing are wide enough to allow considerable room for error or, a better use, to allow experiment and manipulation of the image. Even when the negative has been processed, any number of different images can be made from it, according to the way the photographer treats it in the darkroom when making a print. In this book, we begin with the basic equipment and materials needed to start, look at all the types of film available and how to expose them in different conditions, continue with the graphic possibilities of monochrome, and end with all the procedures needed for developing the film, making enlarged prints and displaying and storing the results. More than in colour photography, doing your own developing and printing is both easy and an essential part of the black-and-white process.

LEFT An historic image of an historic moment. The American space programme used the monochrome image in a colourless environment. The cross-hairs on a plate inside the camera helped to measure and map the lunar surface.

ABOVE Despite its present popularity as the medium of personal expression, it is worth remembering that black and white *was* photography at one stage, and because the materials are so undemanding, black and white is the best beginner's choice.

A taste of the wonderful diversity of the monochrome image: the subject of the picture (**LEFT**), taken in 1926, is the painter Piet Mondrian. The photographer André Kertesz decided to echo Mondrian's linear, unmistakable style in his own composition. The image above, taken by an unknown photographer before the turn of the century, has been toned by the passing of time. Its formal composition achieves a wonderful tranquility; it affects the viewer now, but it is difficult to imagine the shock of such images in photography's infancy. John Thomson is responsible for the image (**RIGHT**) taken in China in the 1860s. 'Responsible' is the right word: the materials and equipment then available placed limitations on everyday, 'candid' photography. The scene is brilliantly posed. For an explanation of the techniques for using daylight indoors (**TOP RIGHT**), see page 52; using natural light can preserve an authentic atmosphere.

Basically, there is no important difference between cameras that can be used with colour film and those that can be used with black-and-white. Although manufacturers have made some improvements with a specific eye on colour photography – colour-matched and colour-corrected lenses, for instance, and exposure metering systems accurate enough for the finer tolerances of colour film – all of these benefit the black-and-white photographer as well. There are no special decisions or choices that you will need to make.

Nevertheless, there remains the question of how far the camera equipment will let you develop ideas and techniques. Camera technology is so advanced nowadays that all current models will make perfectly good images – within certain limitations. The simplest snapshot camera, with a basic lens and using small-framed cartridge film, can produce excellent snapshots – but very little else. Cheap cameras and a small format produce images that are acceptable only when printed small. Also, a camera with one fixed lens allows you a single type of perspective and makes certain kinds of picture out of the question. Wildlife photography, for instance, and most sports, need a telephoto lens to give a magnified view from a distance; including a full view of a room interior calls for a wide-angle lens with a short focal length. If you have only a fixed standard lens, it will limit the range of images you can expect to make.

The sophistication of equipment covers a considerable range and, even if expense is not an issue, the choices need careful thought. The most complex, professional cameras are not always the best – if you do not need the extra facilities and electronics for your kind of photography, these may simply be a hindrance. As a general rule, first decide on your fields of interest in photography, and then look for the equipment that has just enough features for you to get on with it.

Clearly, anyone sufficiently interested in photography to want to learn the entire black-and-white process, from shooting to developing and printing, should also have an adequate standard of camera equipment. The smallest film size that makes any sense is 35mm, and the realistic minimum in equipment is a camera with interchangeable lenses. Most of those available are single lens reflexes, and from now on, the tacit assumption in this book is that you own the equivalent of a 35mm single lens reflex with at least three lenses of different focal length. Over the next few pages, we will look at the essential equipment in more detail.

FAR LEFT No matter whether you are a beginner or a working professional, by far the most convenient format of film to use is 35mm. A 35mm image can take considerable enlargement before any noticeable loss in image quality.

ABOVE LEFT The standard 50mm lens provides your film with a view of the world that approximates to how the human eye sees it. And despite the growing popularity of zooms, most new SLRs still come fitted with a 50mm.

LEFT If wildlife photography takes your fancy, then you will need telephoto lenses. These provide varying degrees of magnification, enabling you to fill the frame with the subject while still keeping out of harm's way.

Viewfinder displays

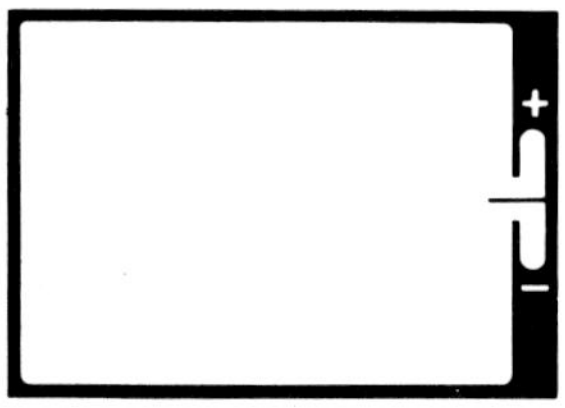
1 Needle

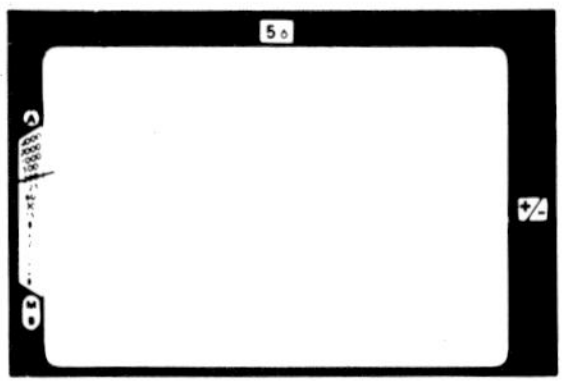
2 Needle Pointer on Scale

3 Digital LED Numbers

4 Digital LCD Numbers

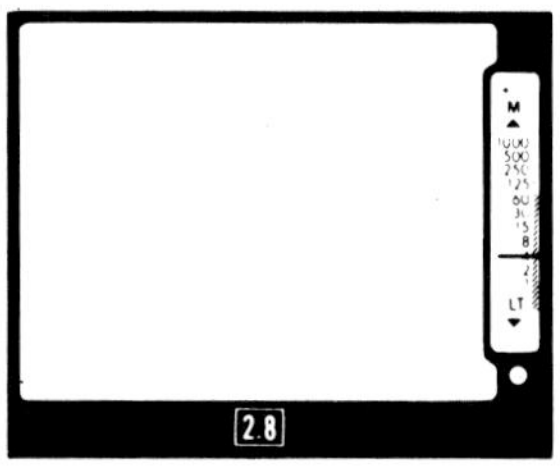

5 LCD Scale

There is now a considerable range of different display systems for conveying essential information in a 35mm SLR, and this has some influence on the choice of camera. A basic difference is between analog and digital displays – as with wristwatches, there tend to be sharp distinctions in individual preference.

CAMERAS

The quality of camera manufacture has never been higher than it is now, and the important choice is not so much between makes as between types of camera. What has happened in recent years in the market is that most of the major manufacturers now produce a similar range of models. Electronics have been the biggest development, and most of the distinctions between categories of single lens reflex are in the extent to which the equipment has been automated.

As things stand at the moment, there are four main types of 35mm single lens reflex, now by far the most popular design of camera for serious photography. The standard current model is automatic, in that the exposure settings are calculated by an internal through-the-lens meter and transferred to the shutter speed and/or aperture controls. Typically, the photographer sets either the aperture or the shutter, and the camera does the rest. Battery-powered film winders are also being used increasingly, so automating yet another function.

An even more sophisticated development of the automatic single lens reflex is the programmed design, pioneered by Canon and Minolta. In this, electronic systems are used to their maximum, all controlled by a central microprocessor. The camera can be programmed to work in a variety of modes, with digital displays playing an important part in the operation. In both automatic and programmed automatic cameras, auto-focus is gradually becoming more and more accepted as a useful function rather than a gimmick. It, also, depends heavily on electronics.

Although automation and programming are clearly the popular trend, there remain many photographers who prefer to exercise their own control over operations – enough for two other types of camera that deliberately avoid heavy automation. These are the manual and professional categories; the first is the more basic, but what distinguishes professional models is their ruggedness and versatility, rather than advanced electronics.

Modes and Meters

Manual In manual mode, the camera measures the light reflected from the subject, and indicates in the viewfinder whether the shutter speed and aperture selected by the photographer will yield correct exposure. The camera is thus totally under the control of the photographer.

Aperture priority automatic (or aperture preferred automatic) In this mode, the photographer sets the camera's aperture, and the shutter is automatically set to a speed that will give the correct exposure. This mode is most useful in conditions where control over depth of field is important – landscape or close-up photography, for example.

Shutter priority automatic (or shutter preferred automatic) Conversely, in this mode the photographer sets the shutter speed and the camera chooses the aperture. This mode is most useful when photographing subjects that must appear "frozen" on film – action and sports photography.

Programmed automatic Ths is a "point and shoot" mode in which the photographer completely relinquishes control to the camera. In progressively brighter light, the camera picks smaller and smaller apertures, and faster and faster shutter speeds. "Sub-modes" include *shutter-preferred programs*, which choose faster shutter speeds before closing down the aperture; and *aperture-preferred programs*, which as the name suggests, pick smaller apertures in preference to faster speeds.

Flash mode In the most simple example, the camera will operate at the flash synchronization speed as long as there is a dedicated flashgun in the accessory shoe, fully recycled.

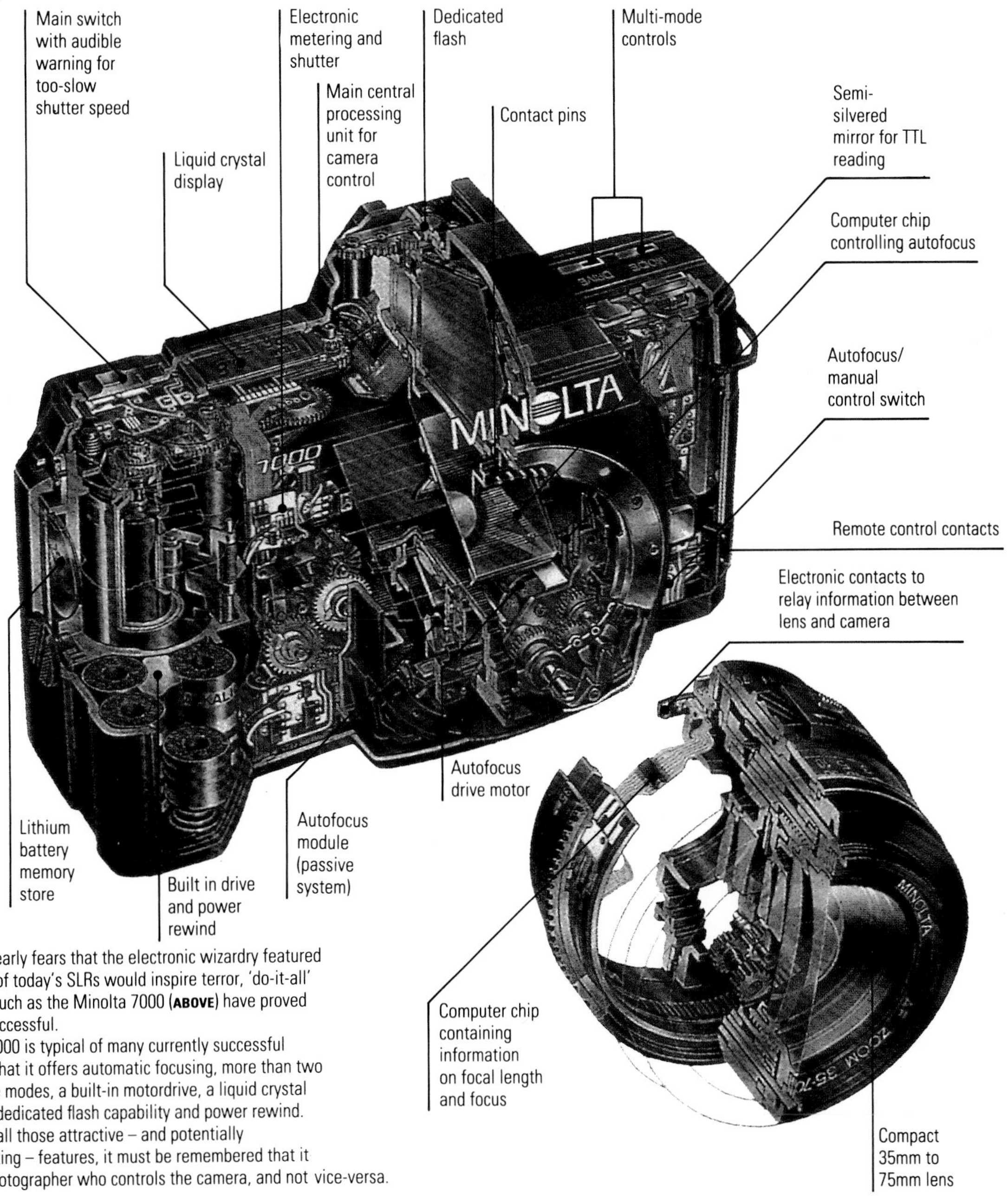

Despite early fears that the electronic wizardry featured in many of today's SLRs would inspire terror, 'do-it-all' models such as the Minolta 7000 (**ABOVE**) have proved highly successful.

The 7000 is typical of many currently successful SLRs in that it offers automatic focusing, more than two exposure modes, a built-in motordrive, a liquid crystal display, dedicated flash capability and power rewind.

With all those attractive – and potentially intimidating – features, it must be remembered that it is the photographer who controls the camera, and not vice-versa.

Apart from single lens reflexes, there are also a few rangefinder models, but now only one that has interchangeable lenses – the Leica MK series. Leica pioneered 35mm photography, and still produces some of the finest cameras available, though they are expensive. Nevertheless, secondhand models are good alternatives.

For simplicity, the examples and advice in this book are aimed principally at 35mm users. However, this is by no means excludes larger formats. Rollfilm cameras that produce images measuring 4.5×6cm, 6×6cm, 6×7cm (and some even larger) are bulkier and usually more expensive, but the image quality is proportionately higher. As the end-result is a finely rendered print, a larger negative is ideal.

LENSES

For all the sophistication of modern camera mechanisms, and the way in which they are heavily promoted, it is the lens that makes the essential difference to the quality and character of the image. As long as the camera, and in particular its shutter, is reliable, there is not much more that you need ask of it, provided that you have some method of measuring the exposure.

Interchangeable lenses, however, offer a world of varied images. While most cameras are supplied with a standard lens – one that has a focal length that gives a normal perspective – you can choose from a range that includes 'fisheye' lenses at one end of the scale to long telephotos at the other. For most people, the major distinction between lenses is in their focal length. This determines the angle of view, and this in turn controls the perspective and magnification.

In the 35mm markets, the choice of lenses is particularly wide, not only because each camera manufacturer produces a range (typically between a dozen and twenty focal lengths), but because there are also independent lens makers. Faced with such a choice, it pays to think carefully about the uses to which you could put extra lenses, and how many you are prepared to carry around. Unless you have a very specific subject of interest that demands an unusual type of lens (such as a long telephoto for wildlife), it makes sense to start with a modest selection. Exotic fish-eyes and shift lenses can come later.

For the time being, we are considering equipment that is basic rather than sophisticated, and it is worth looking at what the most popular focal lengths are overall. For most photographers, the first acquisitions beyond the standard lens (which is usually 50mm) are a moderate wide-angle (around 28 or 35mm) and a moderate telephoto (135 or 150mm). There is no rule that says this is a necessary selection, but this range of three lenses is a first useful step in broadening the range of photographs that you can make.

ABOVE Equipping yourself with zoom lenses can be cheaper, and in some ways gives greater versatility, than choosing fixed focal length models. Currently very popular, 'standard' zooms (top) usually offer a focal length range from mild wide-angle (28mm or 35mm) to mild telephoto (70mm or 85mm), and are normally quite compact. Standard zooms are available that offer greater telephoto magnification, while maintaining their wide angle capability (above). These lenses sometimes exploit their telephoto edge by offering a macro facility (second from top), enabling the photographer to take close-up pictures.

15mm FISH-EYE

24mm WIDE-ANGLE

35mm MODERATE WIDE-ANGLE

50mm NORMAL

180mm MODERATE LONG-FOCUS

400mm EXTREME LONG-FOCUS

600mm EXTREME LONG-FOCUS

800mm EXTREME LONG-FOCUS

1200mm EXTREME LONG-FOCUS

Focal Lengths

This diagram displays the range of different angles of view encompassed by the commonly-available 35mm format. At one extreme, there is the 16mm fish-eye, which takes in almost 180 degrees of the scene – though with considerable circular distortion. At the other extreme is the 800mm telephoto, taking in a mere 3 degrees. The standard 50mm lens falls roughly half-way between, taking in about 40 degrees.

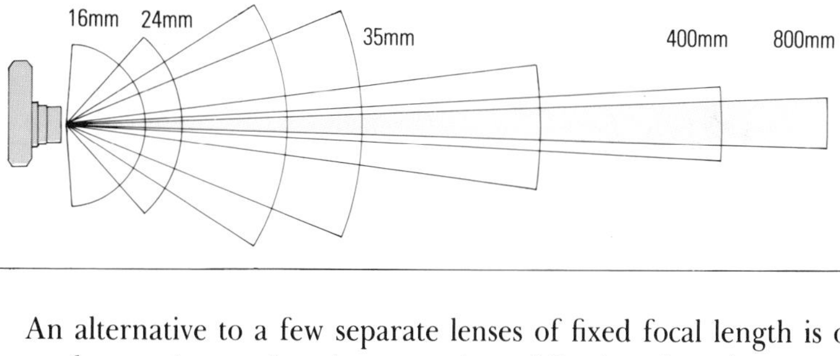

LEFT Modern SLRs invariably accept a bewildering array of lenses. Shown here is just a fraction of the range available for the autofocus Pentax SFX.

An alternative to a few separate lenses of fixed focal length is one or two zoom lenses. A zoom lens has a number of floating glass elements that can be moved to alter the focal length continuously. The ranges vary, but on a 35-70mm zoom, for example, any angle between the two limits can be selected. The advantages are obvious – one lens doing the job of several and an almost infinite choice of framing – but there are also two drawbacks. One is the weight and bulk of the lens, always greater than a fixed focal length equivalent, the other is that the maximum aperture is smaller, and so the lens is not quite as 'fast' as it could otherwise be made. Whether you choose fixed focal length lenses or zooms is a matter of personal preference.

ACCESSORIES & SUPPORTS

Once you have a basic set of camera and lenses, there is a wealth of other equipment to choose from. So much, in fact, that if you were to buy every accessory that seemed useful, you would be so awash in equipment that the actual photography would take second place. This is the principal difficulty with accessories: selecting what is actually necessary and avoiding unimportant gimmicks.

Indeed, even items that are individually a good idea may need to be passed over – there is a low limit to the range of equipment that one photographer can carry and handle at any one time. Here, we ignore most gadgets, however interesting and appealing, in favour of the basic items. Filters, tripods and camera bags may not seem as glamorous or fun as a digitalised data back or remote-control trigger, but they are considerably more useful.

FILTERS

Contrary to the publicity given to special-effects filters such as multiple-image prisms, the useful filters are those that allow you to alter the tones in a normal image. Black-and-white photography is, after all, a matter of tonal values, and anything that enables you to manipulate these is extremely valuable. Filters actually play a more fundamental role in black-and-white photography than in colour, as the effects they have are subtle. The basic film set includes primary and other strong colours, and makes is possible to alter selected tones (a tomato for instance, could be recorded at any tone from near-white to black). All this is dealt with in full detail later in this book. Other useful filters are ultra-violet, for cutting haze; and polarizing, for reducing reflections from non-metallic surfaces and darkening blue skies. All the other filters normally available – light balancing and colour correction sets, are irrelevant in black-and-white photography.

SUPPORTS

While hand-held photography is the norm, there are times when the camera needs to be fixed in position. Low light levels, such as at night and in interiors, call for slow shutter speeds, unless you are using high-speed film. Small apertures to give greater depth of field must also be balanced by longer exposure times. A tripod is the most universal camera support, and repays the effort of carrying it by extending the range of lighting conditions under which you can shoot. Even when there is sufficient light for holding the camera by hand, a tripod helps when it is important to compose a shot precisely, as in architectural photography, for example. It is best to use a cable release with all long exposure times.

BAGS

With a few lenses, spare rolls of film, and some accessories, a shoulder bag is the final piece of equipment. If it has padded compartments, this will protect individual items from damage (and will also obviate any need for an individual camera case). It is usually a good idea to avoid camera bags that are obviously just that; this only invites attention, both from potential subjects in candid photography and from anyone interested in the value of the equipment.

Tripod Heads

Tripod heads should offer the greatest freedom of movement. The basic choice is between the highly flexible ball-and-socket head, and those with separately-controlled movements.

MONOBALL This Arca-Swiss head is the most secure ball-and-socket design available, capable of holding the heaviest 35mm configuration in any position.

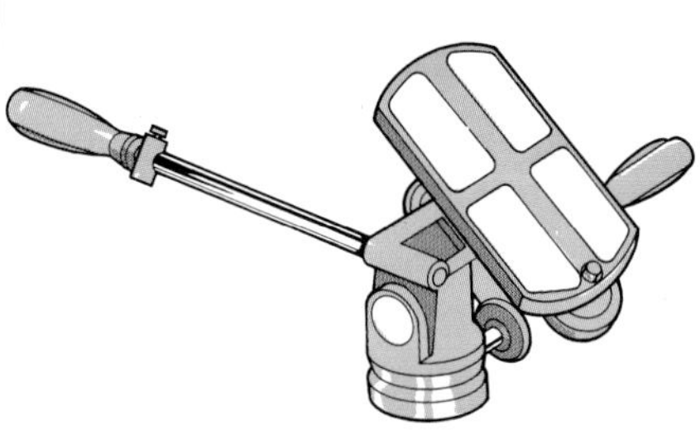

PAN-AND-TILT HEAD Separate movements on this Gitzo Rationelle head allow individual adjustments with greater accuracy.

BALL-AND-SOCKET HEAD Lighter and more common than the monoball, this head is secure enough for most combinations of camera and lens.

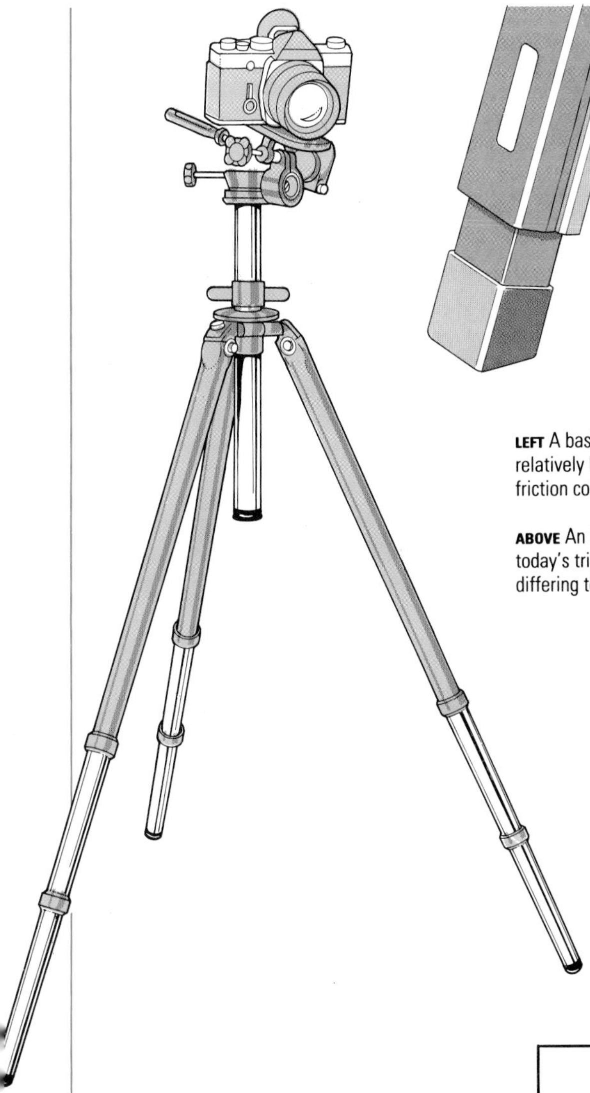

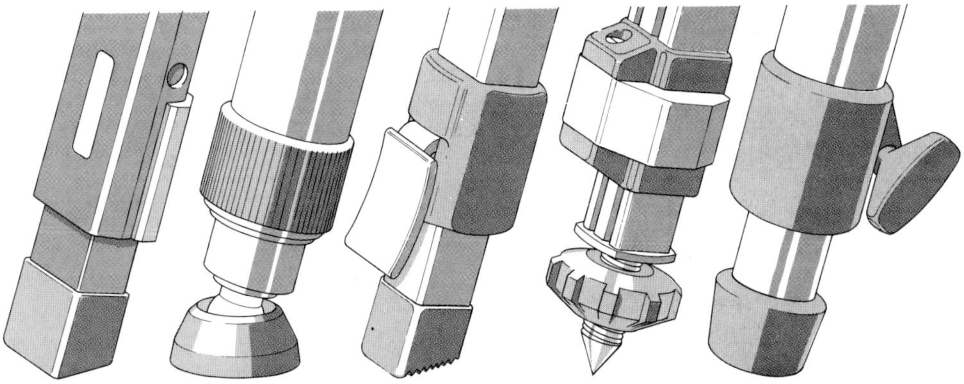

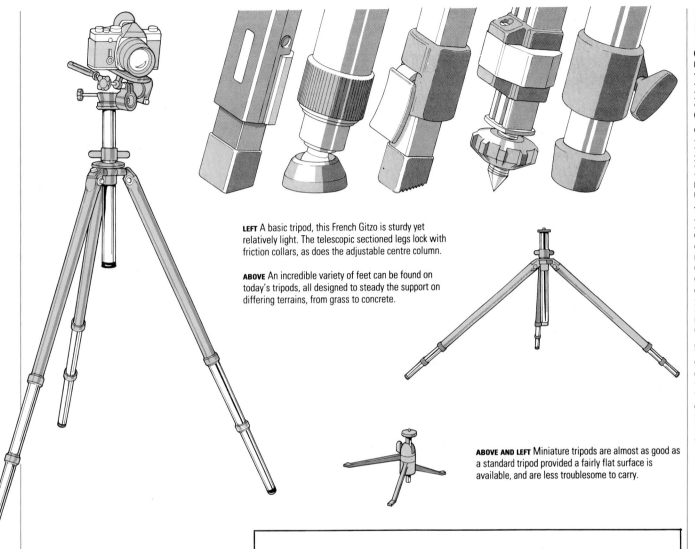

LEFT A basic tripod, this French Gitzo is sturdy yet relatively light. The telescopic sectioned legs lock with friction collars, as does the adjustable centre column.

ABOVE An incredible variety of feet can be found on today's tripods, all designed to steady the support on differing terrains, from grass to concrete.

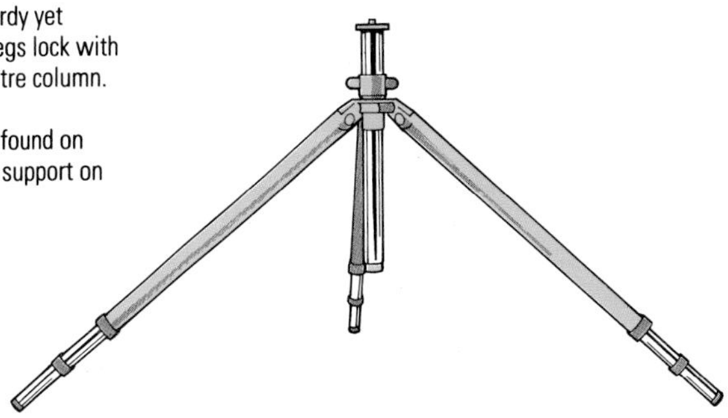

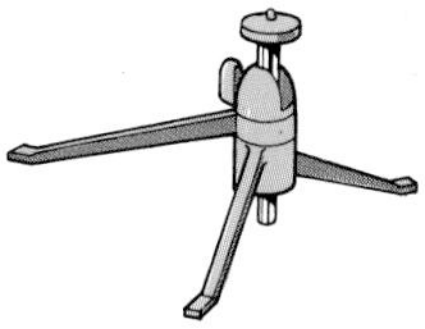

ABOVE AND LEFT Miniature tripods are almost as good as a standard tripod provided a fairly flat surface is available, and are less troublesome to carry.

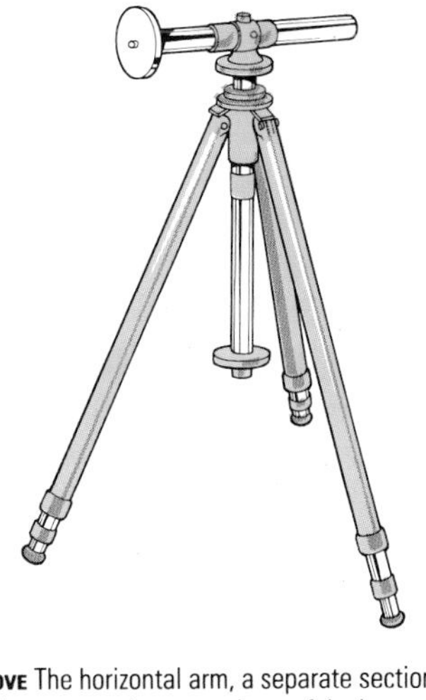

ABOVE The horizontal arm, a separate section attached to the centre column, can be useful when pointing the camera vertically downwards, as in copying.

Camera Bags

LEFT Moulded aluminium camera cases, such as this American Haliburton, are most secure in providing protection for equipment, and are gasket-sealed for protection against grit and water.

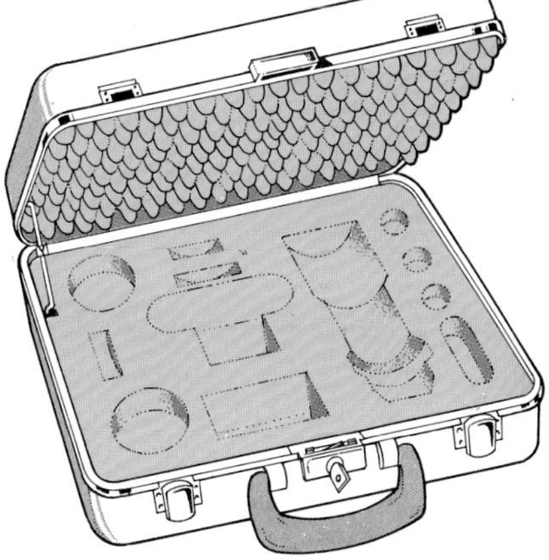

RIGHT Shoulder bags are available in many styles. Separate pockets help prevent equipment from scraping together, while some bags have rigid compartments.

PROCESSING EQUIPMENT

One of the great pleasures in black-and-white photography is being able to follow through the entire process of making an image, from the moment of shooting to the finished print. Arguably, this applies even more to black-and-white than to colour, as the image is more susceptible to control and manipulation. Black-and-white photographers become used to anticipating the darkroom processes even when they are making the exposure: as we will see later in this book, knowing what changes can be made during processing and printing makes it possible to choose exposure settings accordingly.

The immediate stage once a roll of film has been exposed is to develop and fix it, and the equipment and chemicals needed are extremely simple.

Both 35mm and rollfilm are normally processed in a small circular tank, made either of stainless steel or plastic. These are available in different heights, depending on whether one or several films are to be processed at the same time, and the film itself is wound onto a spiral reel. Stainless steel reels load from the inside outwards, plastic reels are grooved for the film to slide inwards, starting at the edge. The lid contains a hole fitted with a light baffle, so that processing solutions can be poured in and out without exposing the film to light. Once loaded, the tank can be used in normal lighting.

Darkness is, however, essential for taking the film out of its cassette and loading it into the tank. The darkroom that you use for printing can double for film loading, but the light-proofing is then even more critical. If you do not have the luxury of a room that can be given over full-time to darkroom use, it is not too difficult to make a temporary conversion of some other room. This is easiest if there is no window, but if there is, it can be blocked out either with a special type of roller blind, or with a solid shutter. A darkroom roller blind fitting is constructed as a box covering the window frame, in which a thick black cloth blind runs inside recessed grooves. The door is another potential source of light: cover the gaps with either draught-excluding flaps or foam strips.

Finally, check the effectiveness of the light-proofing by taking out a short strip of unexposed film, covering part of it with an opaque object, and exposing it in the darkened room for a minute or two. Process it and see if you can distinguish the edge of the object that was covering it; if there is a noticeable

Processing Equipment

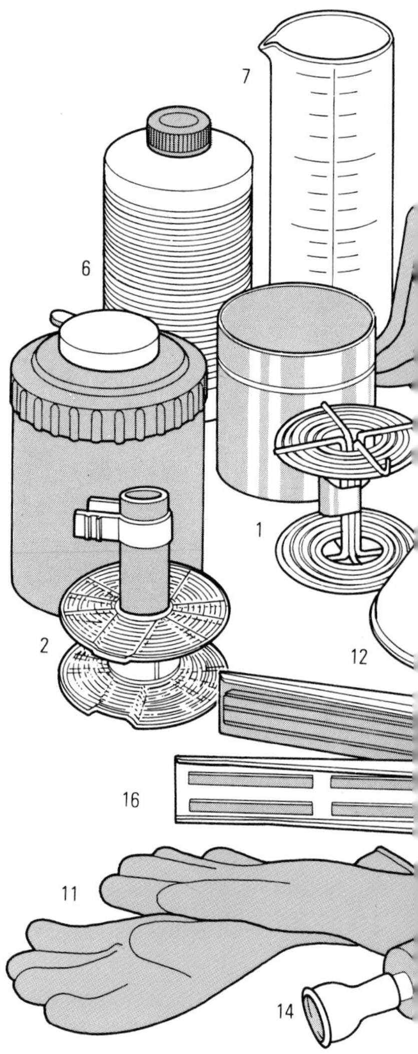

Developing tanks are available in two basic designs – with a stainless steel reel (1), and with a plastic reel (2) which is easier to load but less durable. Developer (3), stop bath (4), and fixer (5) should be kept in clearly-labelled, light-tight stoppered bottles; an even better alternative is an expanding container with a concertina shape (6) which adjusts so that air is excluded. For mixing chemicals, a graduated measuring flask (7) is essential, and to maintain them at a constaint 68°F (20°C) they should be placed in a tray (8) filled with water at that temperature, using a thermometer (9). A

LEFT Standard set-up for black-and-white enlargement.

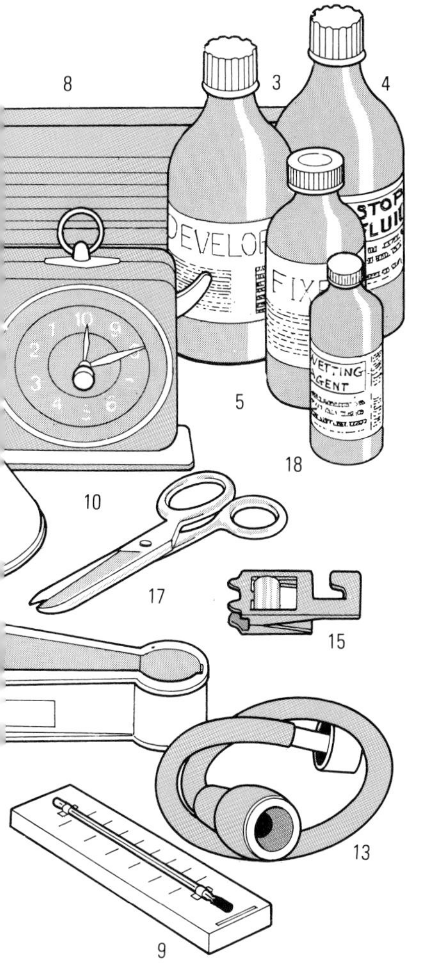

timer (10) can be pre-set to the recommended developing and fixing times. Rubber gloves (11) prevent skin irritation from prolonged contact with the chemicals and a funnel (12) prevents spillage when returning chemicals to the bottles. A water hose (13) and filter (14) are used for washing the film, which is then hung to dry on clips (15). Excess moisture can be removed with a pair of squeegee tongs (16). The film is finally cut into strips with scissors (17). Wetting agent (18) is added to the final wash to help the developer spread more easily and to prevent drying marks.

demarcation of tone, the film has been fogged slightly and the room's light-proofing is not total.

An alternative to a darkroom is a changing bag, which is a double-lined bag of black material fitted with two zips and elasticated sleeves for your arms. Choose one that is large enough to work in easily.

The other equipment you will need is: a bottle opener to open the 35mm film cassettes, scissors to trim the ends, one or two graduates for measuring the mixing solutions (they should be at least as big as the developing tank), storage bottles, thermometer and stirring paddle. Temperature control is by no means as critical as for colour film development, but you will need a source of warm water and a fairly deep tray in which to stand the developer. Clips for hanging the washed film and a clean, dry place in which to hang them complete the list.

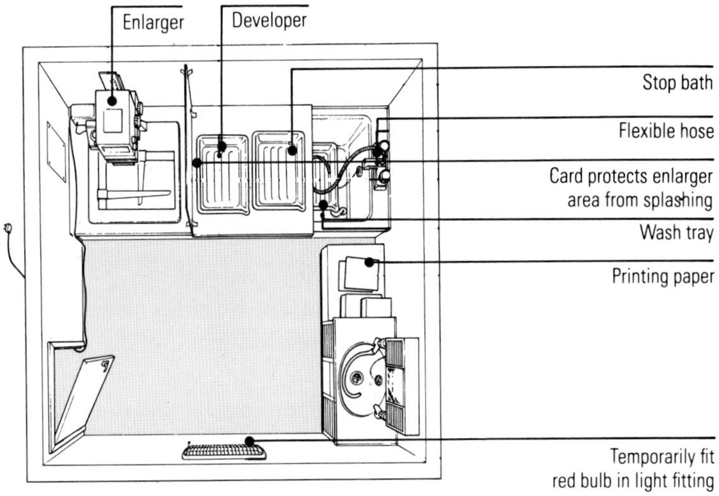

A Makeshift Darkroom

A bathroom has certain advantages for temporary conversion: plumbing, large water containers, and disposal. In the conversion above, a board over most of the bath provides a working surface. Print washing takes place underneath, in the bath itself. Power for the enlarger should be taken from outside the bathroom, for safety reasons.

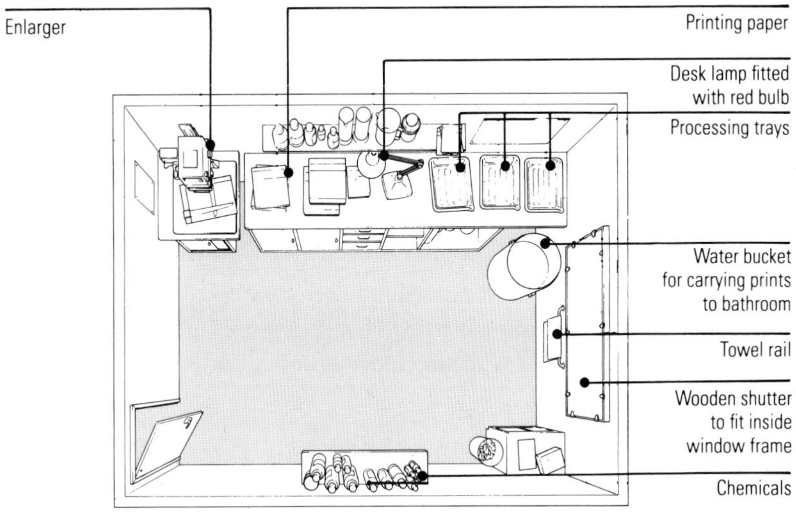

A Converted Study

A slightly more sophisticated type of conversion, yet still temporary, is of an office or study. Even if there is no plumbing, processing solutions can be mixed and brought in from the bathroom, while a plastic bucket can be used for taking fixed prints out for washing. The room can be lightproofed with a wooden shutter that fits tightly into the window frame, and felt or rubber flaps around the door.

ENLARGER & PRINTING EQUIPMENT

Unlike colour, black-and-white photography is geared totally towards printing. With the very minor exception of slides for projection (Agfa make a reversal film, and Polaroid 35mm instant films give a positive image), black-and-white films are only a preliminary stage. The end-product that justifies the effort is an enlarged print. After the camera equipment, the most important item is an enlarger.

Fortunately, a black-and-white enlarger is neither as complex nor as expensive as an enlarger designed for colour printing. There is no need for colour filters (either a red safety filter fitted to some models for swinging in front of the lens, and the filter set used with variable-contrast paper), and the colour balance of the lamp is not so important.

Nevertheless, a good enlarger is a significant investment, and ought to be chosen carefully. First, the size: enlargers are available for all film formats up to sheet film, and the larger sizes will accept all smaller formats. If you think that you might upgrade from 35mm to rollfilm at some point, it is worth getting a medium-format enlarger to begin with. Two focal lengths of enlarger lens will then allow you to print both sizes of negative. As with the camera, what ultimately decides the image quality is the quality of the lens. This is no place to skimp: the enlarger lens should be at least as good as your camera lenses, otherwise you will have wasted their value. For normal enlargements, use a lens that has the same focal length as the standard lens for the format. 50mm or 60mm are the usual choice for 35mm, 80mm or 90mm for rollfilm.

The head of the enlarger contains the light source, and there are two alternative systems: condensers or diffused lamps. In the first, condenser lenses, usually different for each focal length of enlarging lens, focus the light from a small lamp on the negative; in the second, the light is from a large area, and is unfocused and diffuse. Condensers give a slightly sharper and more contrasty image on the print, although they also make the film grain and any blemishes appear more prominently.

An easel is needed to hold the paper in place and give a neat border to the image. The normal design has adjustable masks – strips of metal or plastic – that can be altered for different proportions and sizes. A focusing magnifier focuses on the grain of the negative, and is useful for getting the sharpest possible images.

Contact prints, which are normally made before finished prints as a means of selecting photographs, are made by pressing the negative strips flat against a sheet of printing paper. A sheet of plain glass will do, but a purpose-built contact printing frame is easier to use.

Other equipment includes a red safelight, anti-static brush for cleaning negatives, dodging tools, and processing trays with tongs (if you use different sizes of paper, different sets of trays make more economical use of the processing solutions).

ABOVE AND ABOVE RIGHT There are two basic choices when deciding upon an enlarger head for black-and-white printing; one that features a diffuser lamp, which spreads the light over a large area and is more forgiving, or one which has a condenser lamp, where the light is focused from the small lamp on the negative.

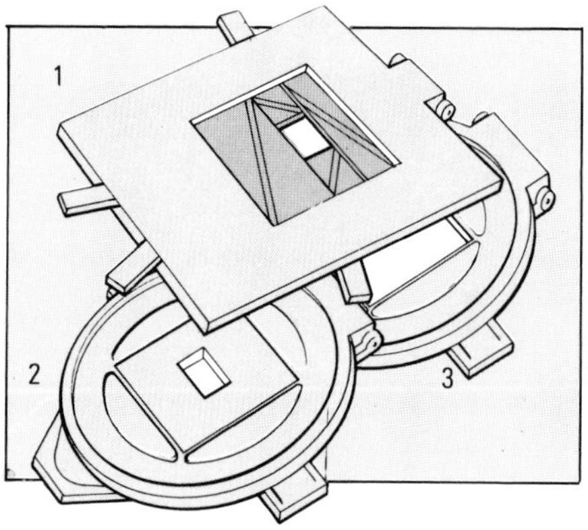

ABOVE Film carrier types include an adjustable mask for different film formats (**1**), a glass carrier to hold thin film flat (**2**), and a hinged plate (**3**).

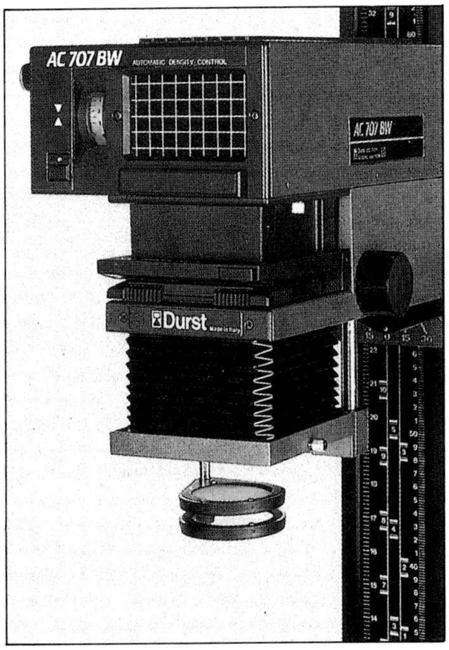

BELOW Black-and-white enlargers tend to be more simple than their colour counterparts, offering a basic means of exposing an image on a negative to light-sensitive paper.

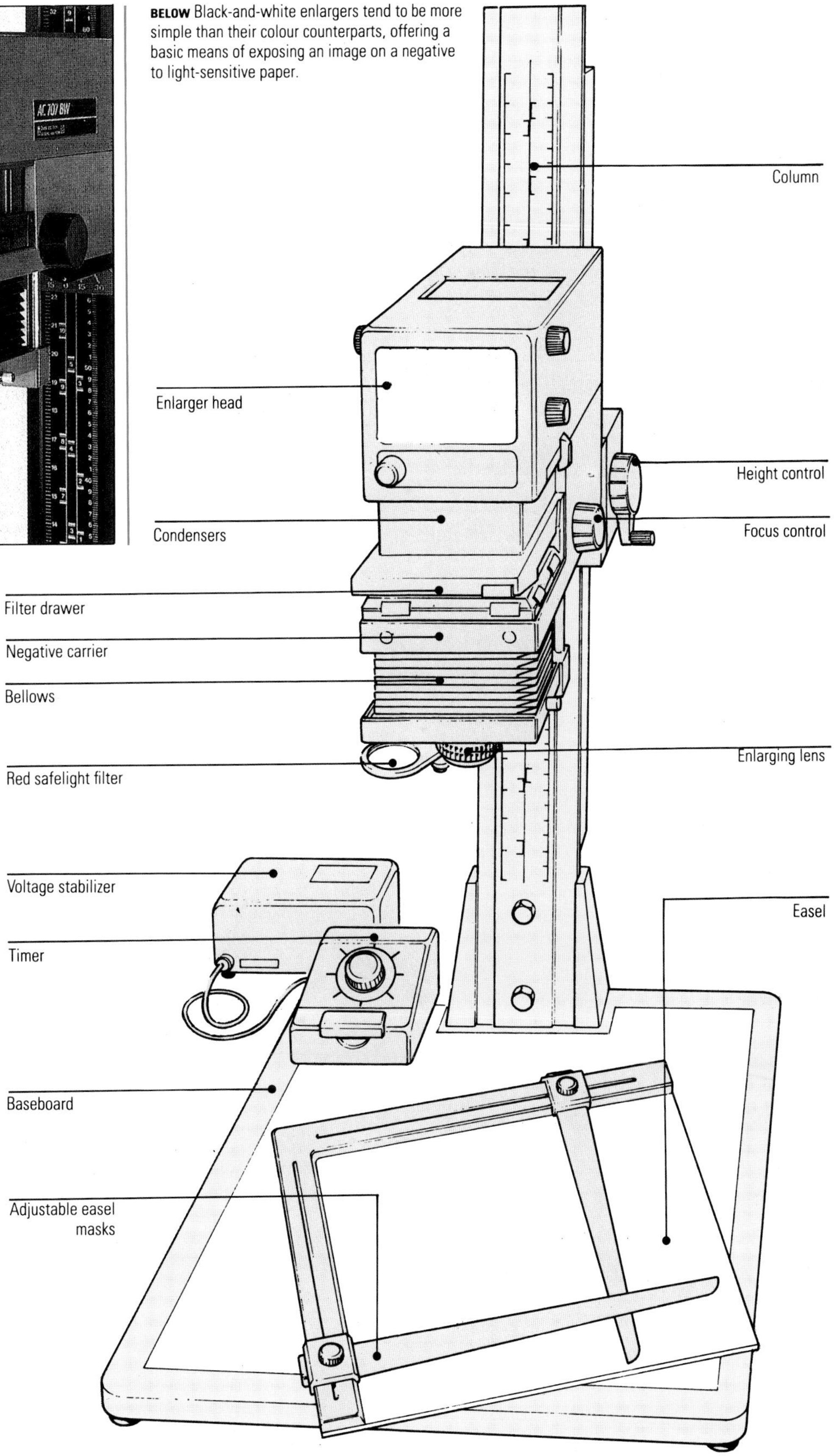

Maintenance Checklist

Check for the following faults:

1. Dirt on the lens. Causes flare and vague dark spots when stopped down.
2. Dirt on condensers or filters. Causes soft-edged dark spots on print at small apertures.
3. Wrong condensers. Make sure they match the focal length of the enlarging lens.
4. Unsteady baseboard. Causes double or blurred image.
5. Torn bellows or gaps in enlarger head. Can cause fogging of print.
6. Condensers badly adjusted. Causes darkenening towards edges of projected image.
7. Wrong enlarging lens. If lens does not cover negative, illumination and image quality fall off toward the edges of the projected image.
8. Focus gears slip. Causes soft focus. Tighten locking screws or relubricate.

OPTIONAL EXTRAS

So far, we have suggested that you acquire just enough equipment to get started, and that you concentrate on learning to use a straightforward selection well, rather than burdening yourself with exotic items that can actually interfere with the process of seeing and capturing images. Apart from anything else, the expense usually curbs most people's appetite for more equipment.

The listings on the earlier pages already represent a fair outlay. If, however, your budget can stand some extra acquisitions, there are some additions that you might like to consider. Nevertheless, start with the basic set.

LENSES

If you want to invest further in your photography, extra lenses are probably the wisest choice. A new focal length will have a direct and immediately visible effect on your work. If you already have a moderate wide-angle and telephoto, you might want to experiment with more extreme focal lengths in either direction. The graphic effects can be unusual and dramatic, but the more extreme the focal length, the more difficult the lens will be to use well and consistently. Expense is normally higher with these extreme lenses and long telephoto lenses can be very heavy.

Very short focal lengths, such as 20mm on a 35mm camera, give spectacular angles of view, which can open up new possibilities in, for example, photographing interiors. Their depth of field is also very good, and this can be used to provide impressive front-to-back sharpness in, say, a landscape. At the same time, they can give pronounced distortion close to the edges, and if you frame the view so that a recognizeable shape, such as a circular object or a face, is in a corner of the image, the result will look odd.

Long telephotos, of 500mm or more, make it possible to select and magnify views that you might not notice with your eye alone. They also enable photographs of things that have restricted access, such as a close view of a tackle in a football match, or an elusive animal. Very long lenses, however, have smaller maximum apertures, and the very expensive fast super telephotos are also extremely heavy and bulky.

Apart from focal length, there are several special designs of lens to allow particular kinds of photography. Fish-eye lenses give the widest coverage of all – some over 180 degrees – but at the expense of strongly curved distortion. Macro lenses are computed to perform best at close distances. Shift lenses (also sometimes designated P-C, or perspective-control) can be moved vertically in their mount, and can be used in architectural photography to shoot tall buildings without tilting the camera upwards and so causing converging lines.

METERS

The other useful category of optional extra is that of hand-held meters. It may seem that these are outdated by the camera's own through-the-lens metering, but in many lighting situations they have distinct advantages. Most hand-held meters permit two kinds of reading: direct, like the through-the-lens meter, and incident. The latter is a measure of the light falling on the subject, irrespective of the brightness of the object being photographed. Perhaps an even more fundamental benefit of a hand-held meter is that it encourages the photographer to think about exposure and to become familiar with light levels – no bad thing if you intend to take a craftsmanlike approach to photography.

The Difference a Lens Makes . . .

Telephoto lenses really come into their own when shooting wildlife; the great magnification offered enables the photographer to remain at a safe distance from the subject, while still filling the frame. The relatively small depth of field common to telephotos also singles out the subject from the backdrop.

When conditions are cramped and you want to get the whole scene in, or when you're simply looking to add drama, fit a wide-angle. The great depth of field will usually lead to photos being sharp from foreground to background, although the more wide-angle the lens, the more the distortion around the edge of the frame.

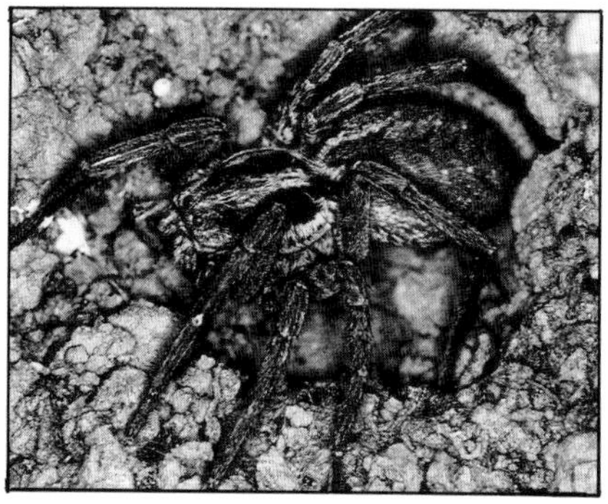

Macro lenses, designed for close-up work, shed a new light on the world. They are particularly useful for photographing insect life, although using a mild-telephoto macro will ensure that you do not scare your subject away. Because depth of field is at a premium, focusing tends to be very critical.

. . . And Why

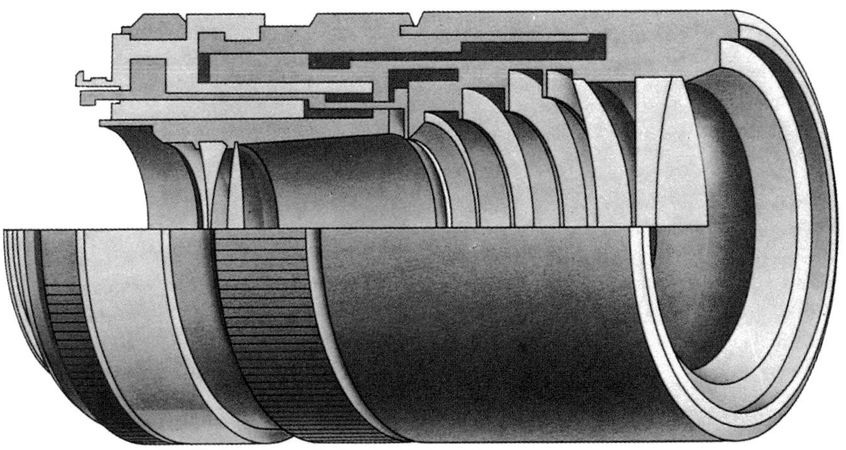

Long focus lenses come in three basic forms. Medium telephotos, such as the one shown left, fall into a focal length range from 85mm to 200mm. They tend to be compact, with the result that they are popular with photographers who work in situations where tripods are inconvenient and it is preferable to hand-hold the lens. Mirror or reflex designs use a combination of mirrors to fold the light path into short light barrels, and invariably offer great magnification. Long telephotos, from 300mm to 800mm, give large magnifications but their weight, and length usually demand that they are used on a tripod.

Wide-angle lenses, such as this 28mm shown left, have obvious applications where the standard 50mm lens cannot fit everything into the frame. Wide-angles tend to be compact, the exceptions being the incredibly cumbersome fish-eyes. The most common maximum aperture found on the most popular wide-angle lenses – 28mm and 35mm – is f2.8, although, at a price, maximum apertures of f2 and even f1.4 are available. The great depth-of-field (distance before and after the point of focus that will remain sharp) offered by wide-angles means that focusing becomes almost a secondary consideration.

Macro lenses vary in focal length from standard (this is, 50mm for a 35mm camera) to medium telephoto (100mm and 200mm are not uncommon).

Good optical quality is easier to maintain with a standard focal length, but the advantage of a longer focal length is that the working distance is greater; for example, you can stay further away from a potentially dangerous subject!

THE SILVER IMAGE

Lacking the element of colour, black-and-white films offer a more limited choice of brands and varieties. However, although this alone might make it more straightforward to select the type and make, the sheer versatility of black-and-white film makes it important to understand how it works – probably more so than with colour film. Textural effects that use the film's graininess, and manipulations of speed and contrast depend on your knowing the characteristics of different emulsions quite well.

Some idea of the basic film process is an invaluable introduction to these different characteristics. The mechanism is this: large numbers of light-sensitive silver halide crystals embedded in gelatin make up the emulsion. On exposure in the camera, those struck by light undergo a very slight reaction – too small to be visible without the help of a developer. Processing magnifies this change several million times: the action of the developing solution converts each exposed crystal to black metallic silver, while those that have received no light remain transparent. The crystals are so small and numerous that they cannot be seen individually without a microscope; the pattern of exposed and unexposed crystals gives a range of tones from almost solid black to nearly clear, with infinite shades of grey in between.

After development, the black silver grains are stable, but the unexposed silver halide crystals are not – any light will turn them black too. To prevent this, the film must be 'fixed' in another solution whch dissolves away the remaining halides; and finally, washed and dried.

The result is a negative image, with all the tones reversed: the bright parts of the original scene make the crystals react and turn black. So, the negative is an intermediate stage in producing a normal, positive image. The printing paper used for enlargements is coated with an emulsion that is similar to that of the film, although less sensitive to light. When the negative is exposed onto this in an enlarger, a new negative image is formed. This time, however, it is a negative of a negative – and so positive.

A black-and-white negative can vary in only a few ways. The most obvious is in how dark or light it is overall, and this is simply a matter of how much exposure the film is given in the camera and how much development in the darkroom. The more of each the film receives, the more of the emulsion will be darkened.

Three other qualities, however, are closely related to the way the film is made. They are speed, graininess and contrast. We will look at each of these in turn in a moment, but it is important to realise that they are all intimately related. The conventional way of making a film more sensitive to light is for the manufacturer to use bigger crystals of silver halide and to stack them in a thicker layer. This means that, when exposed and developed, the black silver grains form bigger clumps, and this becomes visible as a more grainy texture. You cannot have fast speed without some increase in graininess. Equally, contrast is related to speed in that slow films have a higher contrast than fast emulsions.

How Black and White Film Works

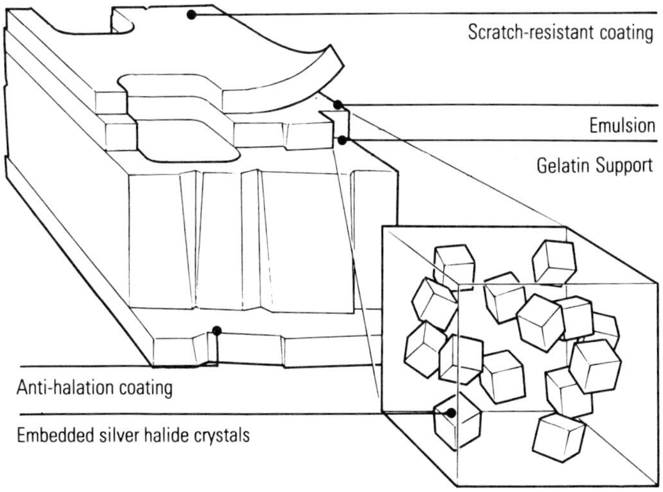

In black-and-white film, the active element is the emulsion – a thin layer of light-sensitive crystals of silver halide suspended in gelatin. This is spread on a tough, flexible but not stretchable base of cellulose-acetate. Protecting the delicate emulsion layer is a scratch-resistant coating, while under the base is another coating to reduce reflection of light back into the emulsion.

1 When black-and-white film is exposed to the light in the camera individual grains that are struck by light react, but invisibly. The mechanism of this reaction is rather more complicated than might at first be imagined, and is triggered by free independent silver ions and small specks of impurities such as silver sulphide. Some of the silver ions collect together at sites that have been exposed to light, forming a latent image. It is called "latent" because, although real, it still needs the action of a developer to increase it in the order of about ten million times in order to make it visible.

2 Adding developer solution to the exposed film converts those silver halide crystals that contain silver ion traces into black silver metal. At this stage, which must be performed in darkness, the crystals that did not receive any light are still sensitive.

3 The final stage in the process is the removal of the developer and the addition of fixer, which turns the remaining silver halide crystals into salts that can be washed away. When this is complete, the image is stable and the film can be exposed to light without any further changes taking place.

LEFT Because black-and-white films that are more sensitive to light use bigger crystals of silver halide stacked in thick layers, fast emulsions feature very noticeable grain. On the other hand, using slow films (as in this example) results in very fine grain and, therefore, higher contrast.

SLOW VERSUS FAST

As we have just seen, choosing a black-and-white film means deciding on priorities, and the principal choice is between film speed and graininess. Were it possible to discount the effects of grain, there would be no need for different film speeds. As it is, there is a range, the fastest being several times more light-sensitive than the slowest.

Film speed depends mainly on the size and shape of the crystals in the emulsion. A large crystal exposed to the same amount of light as a small crystal can be developed just as easily to black silver, and is more visible because of its size. Also, if the grains are flat rather than lumpy, as in some of the latest films, and if these grains are aligned so that the flat side faces the light, they will react more readily. The amount of development and the chemistry of the developer can also be used to make film behave as if it were faster.

In practice, the sensitivity of film is referred to in terms of its speed. An average emulsion – medium-speed, in other words – is one that allows the camera to be used conveniently in most natural lighting. This means a shutter speed of around 1/125sec and an aperture setting somewhere in the middle of the range on the lens. This is a fairly vague definition, and in order to be able to calibrate the camera controls and make accurate exposures, film speed has a standard scale to which all makes now conform. The universally accepted

BELOW Using fast film does not always mean an unsatisfactory graininess as this example shows. Such a photograph would be impossible on slow film.

measurement is the ISO number. ISO stands for International Standards Organisation, and the rating is made up of two numbers. The first is the equivalent of the old ASA figure, the second is equivalent to the system used mainly in Germany: DIN.

A medium-speed film has an ISO rating of between 100/21° and 125/22°. In normal practice, the second figure means so little outside Germany that it is normally dropped.

Film speeds have become standardized over the years, and there are now just three main categories: slow, medium and fast. Slow films are between ISO25 and 32, medium between ISO100 and 125, and fast at ISO400. In addition, there are some specialized black-and-white emulsions with more extreme ratings – for instance, high-contrast lith films rated at around ISO12 and surveillance films rated over ISO1000.

A fast film is more convenient to use in practically every way than a slow film. It can be used in poorer light, allows a faster shutter speed (and so less chance of a blurred image through camera shake) and a smaller aperture (for better depth of field). The only circumstances in which this might not be wanted are if you need a slow shutter speed with shallow depth of field. Nevertheless, choosing the film speed involves other factors, notably graininess, which we deal with in detail next.

BELOW Certain scenes, such as this still-life set, demand that you use a film capable of rendering as much detail as possible. Because of their very fine grain, slow films – between ISO25 and ISO32 – are by far the best choice.

BELOW LEFT On other occasions, you will need to photograph scenes that feature very high contrast; again, slow films' ability to handle high contrast makes them perfect for the job.

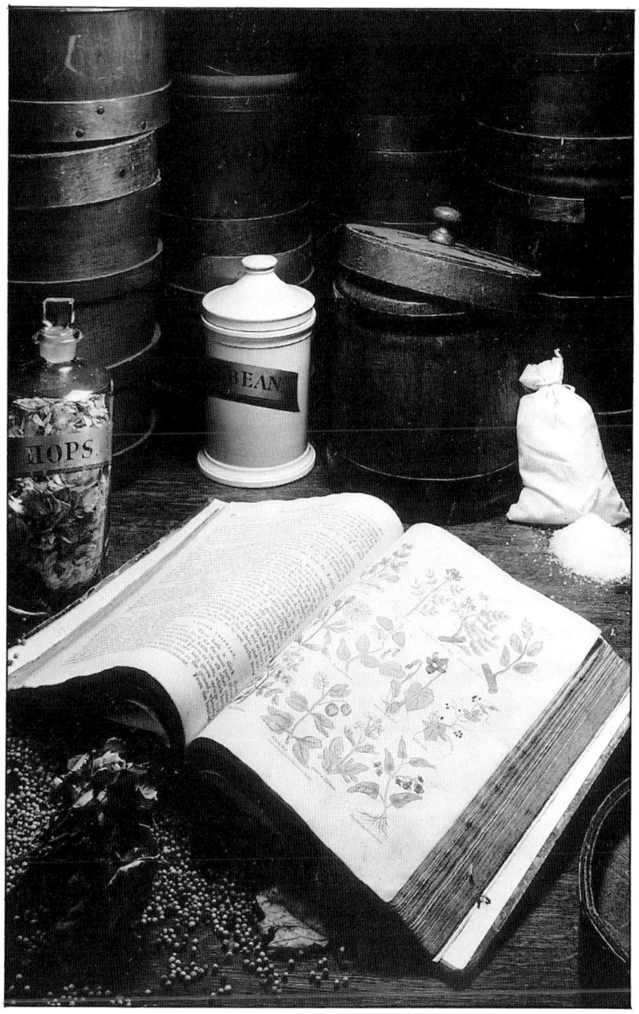

GRAININESS

Graininess is a purely photographic quality. It comes from the process of photography, and not from the scene or subject. Practically, it is one of the most important image qualities, and is more noticeable in a black-and-white picture than in colour. This is because the grains in a black-and-white negative are solid black, whereas developed colour film has instead overlapping patches of transparent dye in three hues, giving a less distinct effect. Whether you consider graininess as interfering with the image or adding to it is a matter of opinion, but how visible it is depends on the type of film, how you develop it, and the degree of enlargement.

The picture opposite shows typical graininess – a speckled texture. What you see here, however, is not the individual grains themselves; they are far too small to be distinguished by the naked eye. Graininess is the appearance of clumps of many grains, overlapping each other in what is a relatively thick layer of emulsion. The grains are jumbled and stacked on top of each other. Nevertheless, graininess reflects granularity, which is the actual measurement of how big and prominent the grains are.

Graininess runs hand in hand with film speed, as is easy enough to see by making a direct comparison between slow, medium and fast film. Photograph the same scene with each in turn; with the only change to the camera and lens being the exposure setting. The difference in the finished print is obvious.

Now, the important result of making this comparison is the most obvious one: graininess only becomes apparent beyond a certain enlargement. The set of full frames printed here from 35mm negatives are not big enough to show any significant difference. This is a valuable exercise to do for yourself, and it will help you in deciding when to use films of different speeds. By experimenting with different enlarger settings, find the degree of enlargement at which you can just detect a grainy texture with each of the three speed categories.

ISO Ratings

Compare the difference in graininess of these three films with different ISO ratings. The print (below left) was taken from the Plus-X film, which has the rating most commonly found.

Panatomic-X, ISO 25; very fine grain

Plus-X, ISP 100; medium grain.

Tri-X, ISO 400; fast, grainy.

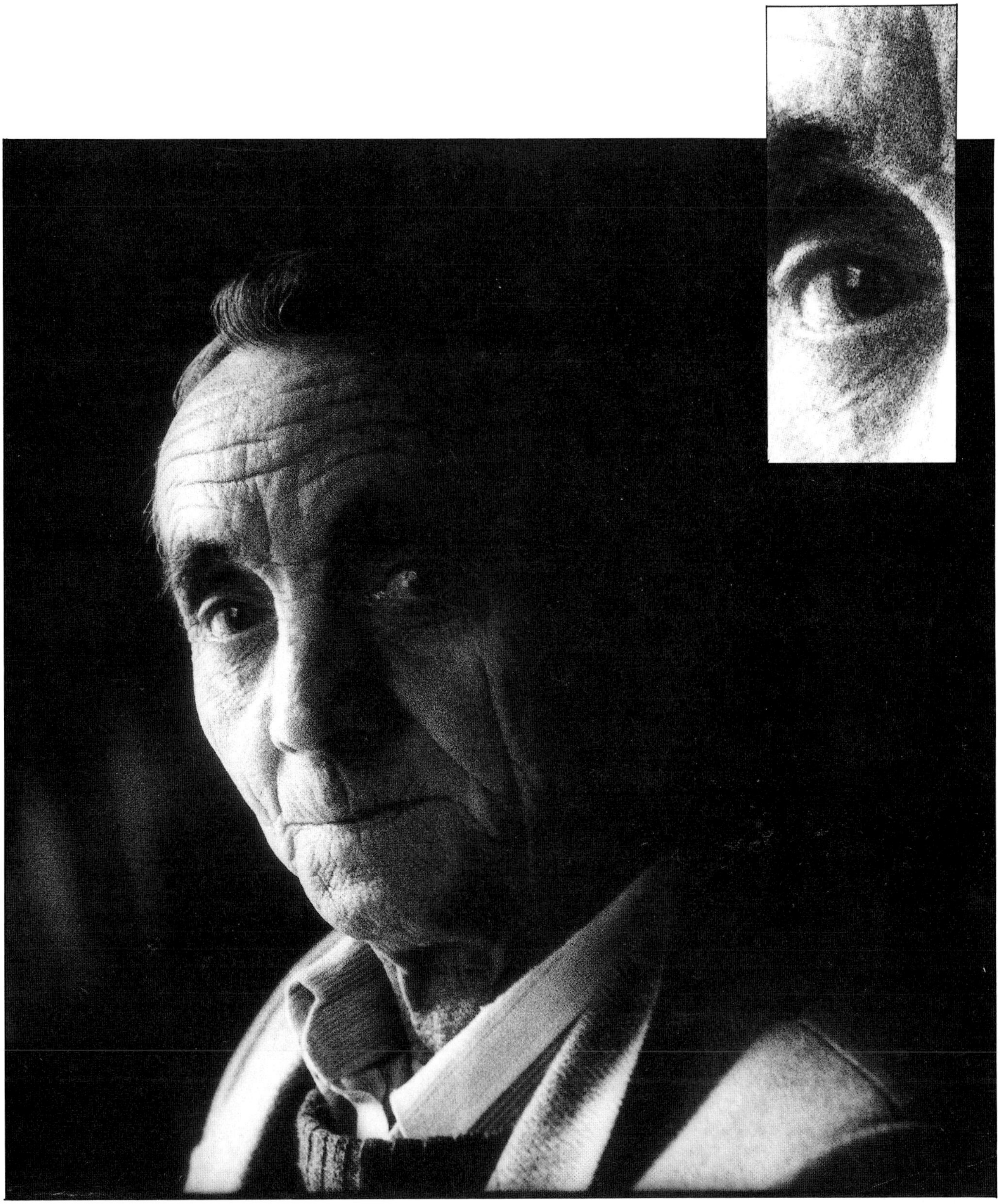

ABOVE AND INSET Graininess creates its own mood, as in this portrait, and should not therefore be seen as inherently detrimental to good prints.

The amount of graininess from any particular film is not necessarily consistent. One other action can affect it: the development. As we will see later, in the section on processing, there are different kinds of developer, and one type is designed to reduce the way in which the silver grains clump together. Known as extra-fine-grain developer, it reduces graininess in any film, although at the expense of speed and contrast. The opposite effect of enhanced graininess occurs if a high-energy developer is used. This is chosen principally to increase the speed performance of film, and makes the grain clumps appear coarser. Over-development increases graininess, under-development reduces it.

ABOVE For most still-life studio shots, graininess would simply be an intrusion, so slower film is the obvious choice.

RIGHT The extremely noticeable grain that is a feature of very fast emulsions can be used to create almost abstract images. In this instance, the camera has been panned – moved to follow the subject – during the exposure, enhancing the effect.

LEFT Although on first impressions a grainy fast film would be the last choice for a portrait picture, the resulting slight softening can be quite complimentary – almost like using a weak diffusing filter. Also, the grainy look can add atmosphere to a candid portrait, such as the one shown here.

GRAININESS

From a purist approach to photography, graininess should be avoided; it overlays the image, and on a small scale breaks up detail. If the ideal is a perfectly resolved, smoothly toned image, grain is an intruder.

For the most part, this holds true. Most of the techniques and skills in photography are, after all, to do with making the best possible likeness of a scene or subject. Nevertheless, this is no rule, and there are occasions when you might feel that the texture of grain enhances the photograph. There is room in photography for all kinds of imagery beyond the traditional and conventional.

First, however, look at how and where graininess has its effect. If you think of it as a kind of speckled screen that is combined with the negative image, it becomes obvious that graininess will be more prominent in a featureless area of the film. Wherever there is a lot of fine detail, and particularly if this is crisp and contrasty, any graininess gets obscured. On a blank part of the image, however, there is only graininess – at least, as long as the tone is grey. In a completely transparent part of the negative (this will print black) there are no developed grains, while in a dense area (a highlight on the print) the grains are so heavily clumped together that there is virtually no texture.

Graininess can have a positive effect, paradoxically, on sharpness, The reason for this is that sharpness is another subjective quality – an impression built up from things like resolution and acutance. While in one sense large grain clumps break up edge detail and work against the impression of being sharp, the specks of grain themselves appear crisp, and if they are in a distinct and even pattern, they can help the overall sharpness. This is one reason why many black-and-white photographers who are accustomed to working with fast film (photojournalists, for instance) have distinct preferences in the make of film they use – there are subtle differences in the grain texture between brands.

Depending on the photographer and on the occasion, the gritty appearance of a grainy print may even be attractive. In the same way that fog, mist, backlighting and certain filters help to create atmosphere in a photograph rather than sharp realism, so a strong grain texture can give an impressionistic effect.

Slow films tend to offer higher contrast, although using an extra-fine-grain developer tends to have the effect of lowering that contrast (top).

CONTRAST

The third related image quality is contrast. When used to describe the performance of a film, this is a measure of how the range of tones in the negative compares with the range of tones in the real scene. Although this is reasonably straightforward, contrast is highly manipulable.

Imagine a typical daylit scene, with a full range of intermediate tones, some shadows and some highlights (ignore the colours). With a meter, you could measure the range of tones; there would probably be a difference of several stops between the lightest and darkest parts. A film that, given the correct exposure, reproduces all these tones more or less exactly has medium contrast. This, indeed, is what happens with a regular medium-speed film: if you take care over the exposure, processing, choice of paper grade, and printing, the final print should have the same tonal range.

However, contrast is linked to speed and graininess, and slow emulsions are more contrasty than fast. This is complicated a little by the processing stage: an extra-fine-grain developer, or under-development with any other, tends to lower contrast, while high-energy developers or over-development increase it.

These contrast differences affect the negative image but, unlike graininess which is transmitted faithfully from the negative to the print, the amount of contrast also depends on the printing stage. In practice, contrast differences between types of film and methods of development are much less than those that can be made later, in the darkroom. As we will see in the section on printing, the selection of printing paper grade, dodging and burning-in techniques and print development can cover most of the film differences.

If you examine a negative carefully with a magnifier, and then a straightforward print is made from it, you will notice that there is more highlight and shadow detail recorded in the negative than in the print. This is because the volume of the transparent gelatin in which the grains are embedded prevents absolute blackness, while in the unexposed areas gelatin and film base together give a pale grey tone. A print, on the other hand, is viewed by reflected light, so that the black silver grains that form the shadow areas have a double effect (they block light falling on the paper and that reflected from it). The highlights in a print can be as bright as the coating, which is deliberately chosen for its whiteness.

Note how there is more shadow and highlight detail in the negative (below) than in the straightforward print produced from it (above).

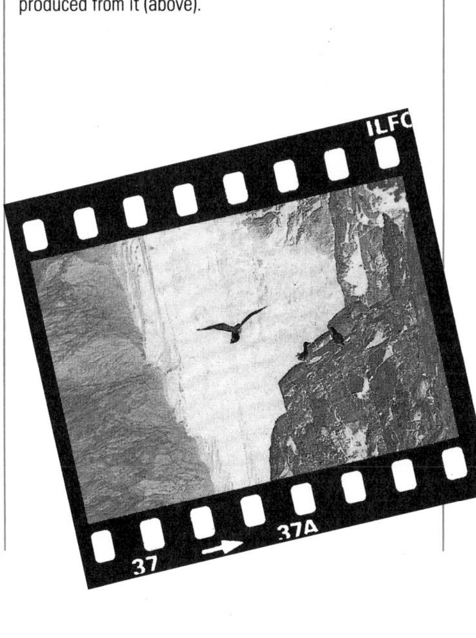

FORMAT

The camera you use will determine the size of film you buy, and with 35mm there is no further choice. All 35mm cameras accept the single, standard film width, and with few exceptions (half-frame and panoramic models) the negative frame is a standardized 24×36mm, that is with proportions of 2:3.

With medium and large format cameras, however, there is often a choice of frame size, and this has a significant effect on the image quality. Graininess, as we saw earlier becomes apparent only beyond a certain degree of enlargement. If you normally print up to 8×10in, a 35mm negative will need to be enlarged 60 times to fill the paper, but a 6×7cm negative only has to be enlarged just over 12 times. At the extreme, a large-format 8×10in negative shot on a view camera would need no enlargement at all: it could be contact-printed for the finest image quality of all.

View cameras, however, are really outside the scope of this book. Medium-format cameras accept 6cm-wide rollfilm, and this is large enough to allow some choice of frame sizes. 6×4.5, 6×6, 6×7, 6×8 and 6×9cm are all possible formats, some of them available as alternatives on the same camera by using different film magazines. Panoramic frames, though used much less often, are even longer.

The degree of enlargement, and so the image quality, depends also on another factor: the proportions. Printing paper and negatives do not always have the same shape. A 35mm negative is significantly more elongated than the typical 4:5 proportions of printing paper. To use the whole of the print, a negative must be cropped, and so enlarged even more; alternatively, printing the entire 35mm negative wastes some of the paper. 6×4.5 and 6×7cm formats on rollfilm are almost matched to the paper, so that if you compose the original shot to the limits of the viewfinder frame, and then print up the entire negative, this is the most efficient use of film and paper.

LEFT An advantage that the 6 × 7cm format shares with the 6 × 4.5cm, is that when enlarged the formats on rollfilm almost match the printing paper. Therefore, the minimum amount of image loss results.

TOP Although the half-frame format has never come close to the roaring success of 35mm, it has recently experienced a revival with the release of cameras offering both 35mm *and* half-frame. The format's name is self-explanatory; it is half a 35mm frame.

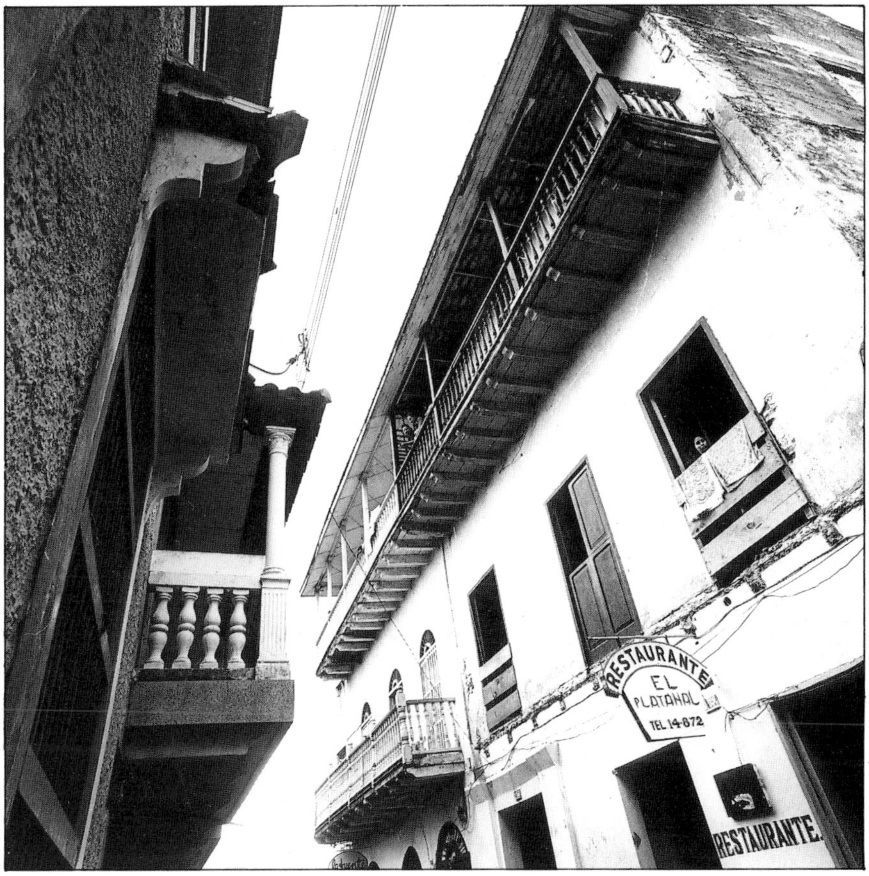

ABOVE The 35mm format is undoubtedly the most popular in the world – and shows no signs of decline. However, when composing a picture on 35mm film, you must always remember that a certain amount of the image will be lost when printed, due to the mismatched proportions between 35mm and normal printing paper.

RIGHT As with 35mm, a certain amount of a 6 × 6cm frame will be lost during normal printing, because of paper sizes and proportions. However, the 6 × 6cm format does open a world of challenging possibilities to the photographer interested in unusual composition.

Film is also available in different lengths. Black-and-white 35mm is sold in cassettes of 36, 24 and 20 exposures. Longer lengths are more economical, but if you are using a special film for one occasion, you may need fewer frames. The most economical of all ways of shooting 35mm film is to buy it in bulk and load it yourself into empty cassettes. This has the added advantage of allowing you to cut short lengths, according to need.

Rollfilm is available in two forms: 120 and 220. The difference is that while 120 has a paper backing and gives 12 frames per roll with a 6×6cm camera (less for the larger frame sizes), 220 has no paper and so can be wound tightly enough onto the same size of spool to allow twice the number of frames.

COLOUR SENSITIVITY

Colour depends on the wavelength of light – and on the way in which the human brain has become accustomed to interpret it. Redness or blueness are simply the ways in which we recognize specific wavelengths.

Black-and-white film does not actually show colour in this familiar way, as different hues, but it does record all the same wavelengths. A black-and-white print then displays the colours as different tones of grey; but as the originals can also be bright or dark, most original colours can turn out in any shade.

This, however, only causes confusion when the object is unfamiliar. With something obvious, memory fills the gap – we simply assume, for instance, that grass in a monochrome photograph is green, however dark or light grey it looks. One of the special advantages of black-and-white photography is that the darkness and lightness of coloured objects can be altered with filters.

In normal ways, however, black-and-white film has a particular response to different wavelengths, and it is not perfect. Neither, however, is the way our eyes see, and what film manufacturers have tried to do, by using special dyes in the emulsions as filters, is to match the response of human vision.

Light is simply visible wavelengths; it is, in other words, what we can see. There is much more radiation shorter and longer than the wavelengths represented by colours: ultra-violet is shorter than blue and violet, infrared is longer than red, and both are invisible. Our eyes have the best response in the middle of the scale of colours, to yellow-green, and the least to violet and deep red.

The silver halide crystals that form the basis of all film emulsions unfortunately have a different response. Used without special treatment they are very sensitive to blue and hardly react at all to red. In the darkroom, when printing, this is helpful, because the paper can be handled perfectly safely in a red light bright enough for comfortable vision. When shooting scenes with a camera, on the other hand, this would be a serious problem, upsetting the expected tonal balance. Indeed, in the early days of photography, it was such a problem that

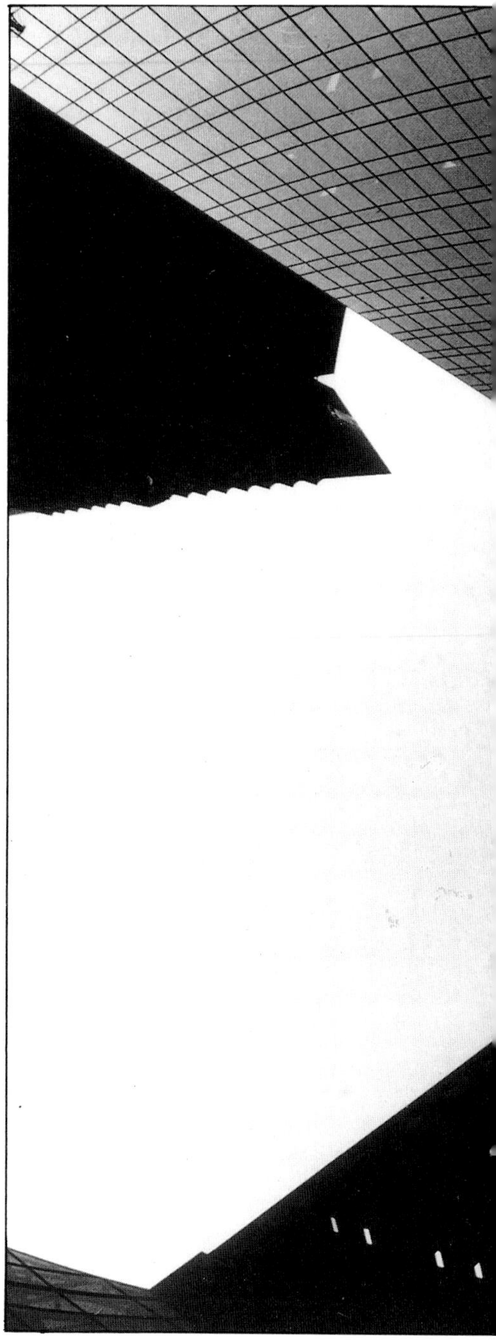

FAR LEFT Without special treatment, black-and-white film usually renders blue skies far blander than we remember them.

LEFT However, the situation can be improved with the use of an orange or yellow filter fitted to the lens. The choice of filter depends upon the strength of sky required; orange will give a dramatic, deep sky, while yellow will give a more 'realistic' rendition.

white skies and dark flesh tones were typical. Clouds in a blue sky were rendered virtually invisible, because the blue exposed so strongly, to the point where it became common practice to add skies to a photograph from another negative.

Modern black-and-white film overcomes most of this with built-in filters to even out this sensitivity, and so is called 'panchromatic'. Still, some of the old skewed response remains, and blue skies still appear paler than visual memory. Some special emulsions that are intended to be used under red darkroom safelighting, such as lith films, are deliberately left insensitive to red – they are called 'orthochromatic'.

ABOVE Silver halide crystals are very sensitive to blue and hardly react at all to red without special treatment. In the early days of photography, skies used to be added to pictures from other negatives, although these days the problem can be resolved with filters.

SPECIAL FILMS

Apart from the normal, limited ranges of black-and-white emulsions, there are a number of others made for special purposes. While none of them could serve as a photographer's regular film stock, they are ideal for certain specific situations. In addition, simply by producing a different kind of image, they can be valuable for occasional use as a means of injecting new graphic interest into an image.

KODAK RECORDING FILM 2475

Rated at ISO1000, this special emulsion is designed for low-light photography, sacrificing quality for the ability to record an image. It is extremely grainy, even at a small enlargement, and has extended red sensitivity for better performance with available tungsten lighting, which is orange.

ILFORD XP-1

This is a chromogenic film, that works on a similar principle to colour negative emulsions. The original silver image is replaced with dyes, to give an image free of the traditionally distinct grain. More importantly, it has a much greater latitude than normal silver-image films, and can tolerate massive under- and over-exposure. It needs to be processed in colour negative chemicals, however, or its own special developer.

AGFA DIA-DIRECT

With reversal processing, this slow (ISO32) emulsion gives a projectable monochrome-transparency, intended for use in slide shows.

ABOVE Kodak's High Speed Infrared film has extended sensitivity beyond the longest visible wavelengths. With a 25 red filter, as here, scenes look more natural than if a visually opaque filter were used. Most lenses feature a red focusing mark on the barrel for use with infrared film.

LEFT When used with the appropriate high-contrast developer, Lith film produces a negative that has only two tones; clear and black. The film can be used to print, for example, silhouettes. Varying exposure simply alters the relative proportions of black and white in the image.

FAR LEFT An image captured on Ilford XP-1, a chromogenic film related to colour negative emulsions. XP-1 can take massive under-and overexposure and still result in images with relatively fine grain. However, it needs to be processed in colour negative chemicals.

INFRARED

Kodak's High-Speed Infrared has extended sensitivity beyond the longest visible wavelengths. When used with a visually opaque filter (Wratten 87 or equivalent), it can give startlingly unusual renditions. Certain surfaces and materials reflect infrared wavelengths quite differently from visible light, so that on this film they appear lighter or darker than expected. Healthy green vegetation, for example, is very bright, while blue sky is almost black. With a 25 red filter, or none at all, the visible wavelengths dominate, and the results look less unusual.

High-Speed Infrared film is not easy to use. It needs careful storage (at low temperatures) and protection from light to the extent that even the cassette should only be handled in darkness. Most lenses are not perfectly corrected for chromatic aberration, and focus infrared rays at a different point from ordinary light; be careful to use the red focusing mark provided for this purpose on the barrels of most such lenses. The emulsion also has a very coarse grain.

LITH FILMS

These are, strictly speaking, not designed for normal camera use, but can give interesting and dramatic results if you do. They are intended for various kinds of special darkroom procedure; used with the appropriate high-contrast developer, they produce a negative that has only two tones: clear and black. This film can be used for slide projection (the best way of making titles) or printed to give, for example, perfect silhouettes. Varying the exposure simply alters the relative proportions of black and white in the photograph; there are no intermediate tones.

ABOVE A typical example of Polaroid's high-contrast monochrome slide emulsion.

INSTANT FILMS

For 35mm cameras, Polaroid makes a black-and-white transparency film of medium speed and a normal range of contrast, and also a high-contrast monochrome slide emulsion. The film handles as any regular emulsion; it is supplied in standard cassettes which are loaded, exposed and rewound as any other, and are the newest type of instant film.

Apart from carrying a positive image rather than a negative, the main point of difference in Polaroid 35mm film is that it is exposed through the base of the film rather than through the emulsion side. This means that, when viewed the right way round, these black-and-white transparencies have their delicate emulsion layer facing towards you. Beware of sliding a loupe across the surface of the film; the emulsion scratches easily. If your camera has an off-the-film metering system, test its performance with this instant film as this kind of metering normally relies on a matt film surface, and the shiny film base may cause incorrect readings.

Processing is straightforward, clean and rapid, but requires Polaroid's own processing unit (there is a hand-cranked or a powered version). The chemicals are provided individually with each roll of film in a sealed box which is discarded after use.

The high-contrast Polagraph is different from conventional lith films in both

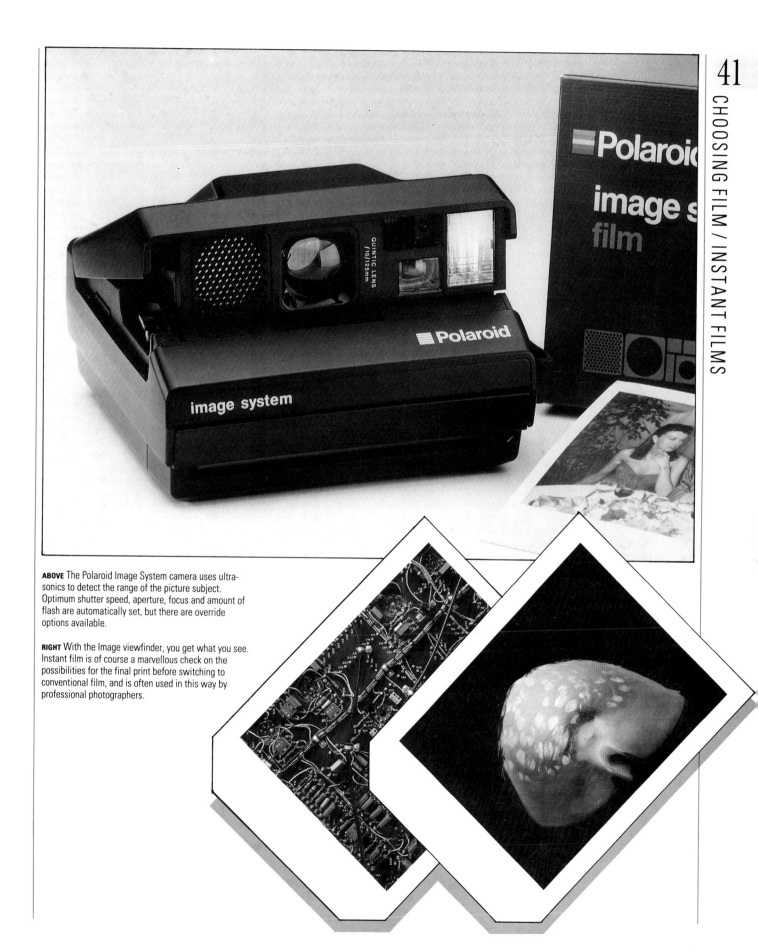

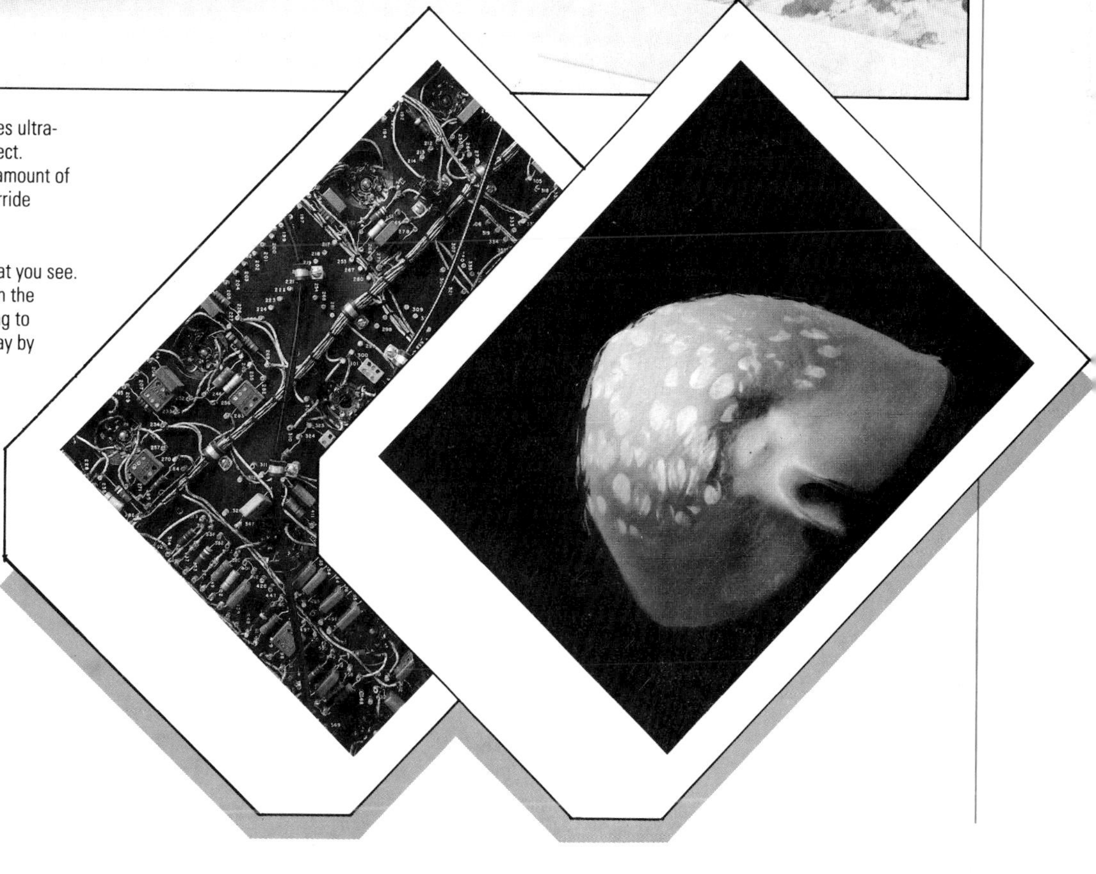

ABOVE The Polaroid Image System camera uses ultrasonics to detect the range of the picture subject. Optimum shutter speed, aperture, focus and amount of flash are automatically set, but there are override options available.

RIGHT With the Image viewfinder, you get what you see. Instant film is of course a marvellous check on the possibilities for the final print before switching to conventional film, and is often used in this way by professional photographers.

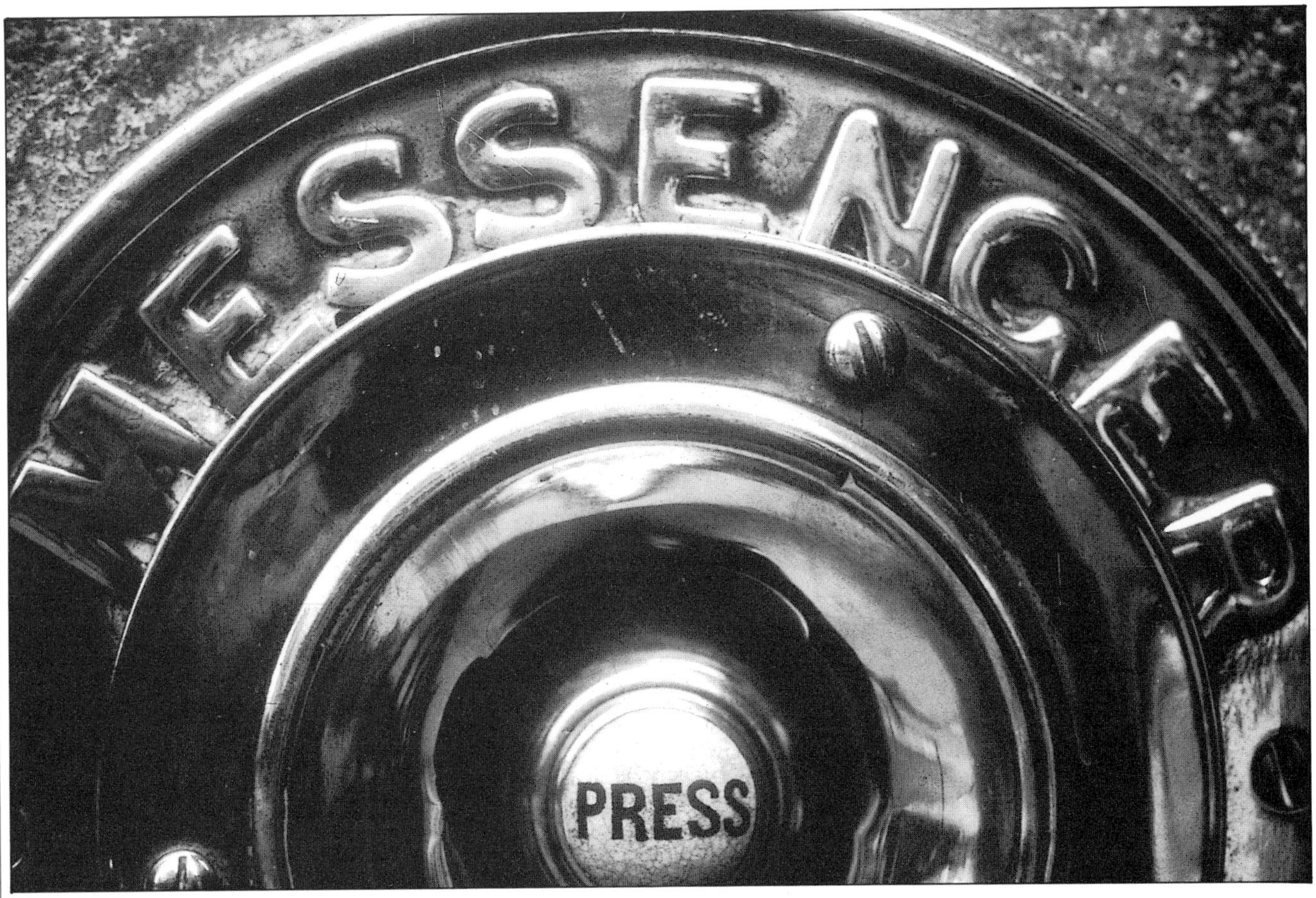

ABOVE PolaPan film gives a positive monochrome 35mm image, and is suited to use in a normal SLR. However, when not backlit PolaPan slides appear to be negatives!

being positive and being panchromatic. As it is as sensitive to red as normal emulsions, it is more suitable for normal camera use.

The other, older varieties of instant film produce prints as an end-product and must be loaded into special holders to fit on medium-format or large-format cameras, or must be used in special Polaroid Land cameras. There is a normal-contrast, medium-high speed film (Types 552 and 52, medium-format and 4×5in respectively), a high-contrast film (Type 51, 4×5in), a high-speed film (Types 87, 107 and 57, the first two medium-format, the last 4×5in), and a fine-grained normal-contrast film that produces a high-quality negative in addition to the print (Types 665 and 55, medium-format and 4×5in respectively).

These are peel-apart films; after exposure, they are processed by first being drawn through a set of metal rollers (which squeeze out a pod of chemicals), then the print is peeled away from the remainder of the thin packet. The processing times and temperature differ from film to film, and are given on each pack.

The most popular use of instant films among professional photographers is as a form of testing. With an important shot, or one that carries some uncertainty, such as in the exposure setting, it is a simple matter to make a test shot on one of these instant films first. Then, if necessary, any changes can quickly be made before shooting on regular film. The positive-negative films types 665 and 55, however, offer a greater benefit to the black-and-white photographer. The negative is very fine-grained and immediately verifiable – a valid alternative to normal black-and-white film.

CAREFUL FILM USE

In most ways, black-and-white film is more rugged than colour, with more exposure latitude and less susceptibility to ageing and poor storage. Nevertheless there is no reason to be sloppy in the way you treat it: all film is perishable and gives its best results if kept in the recommended conditions and processed as soon as possible after it has been exposed.

ABOVE Silica gel is a dessiccant that soaks up moisture from the air like a sponge. Pack it with film and equipment if the humidity is high (but not in dry heat as it will then make the film brittle). For the best drying effect, use airtight cases and pack them tightly so that there is little empty space. One ounce of silica gel will keep nearly 1 cubic ft (0.3 cubic m) of air dry. It can be dried in an oven for reuse.

STORAGE

As film ages, it slowly loses both sensitivity and contrast. This is an admittedly slow process with black-and-white film, but it happens even so. Part of the information printed on the box is the date by which it should be used, and this applies if the film is kept under 'normal' conditions – room temperature and moderately dry air. Two things accelerate this ageing process: heat and humidity. Be careful in either condition to avoid keeping unprocessed film for long; when the two are combined, the film ages even more rapidly.

Conversely, cooling film slows down the ageing process. To keep film almost indefinitely, seal it in a moisture-proof container (the 35mm film can will do) and put it in the freezer compartment of a refrigerator at −18°C (0°F) or below. When you are ready to use it, allow enough time for it to reach room temperature before opening the container, or else moisture is liable to condense onto the film itself.

A more generally useful storage method is in an ordinary refrigerator at about 4°C (39°F). Again, allow time for it to warm up before use.

CARRYING FILM

On a trip, storage conditions are likely to be less than ideal. Keep the film out of direct sunlight, below 16°C (60°F) for as much of the time as possible, and at a relative humidity of less than 60%. In really hot sticky weather, an insulated container such as a styrofoam picnic box is a good idea, and a packet of silica gel crystals will keep the air inside dry.

X-RAYS

X-rays are radiation – like light but a much shorter wavelength – and will fog film if the dose is high enough. Nearly all airports now use X-ray security machines, and while most are designed to give a dose that is too small to harm film, the effect is cumulative. So, if you carry the same film through several airports, it may receive enough X-rays to fog it. Also, high-speed films are more susceptible than regular emulsions. Black-and-white films, fortunately, suffer less than colour, but try and avoid letting them pass through machines. In the United States you are entitled to ask for a hand-inspection, but in other countries this is not always possible. Lead-lined bags sold in photo stores give some protection, and checked baggage for the hold is far less likely to be subjected to X-ray inspection.

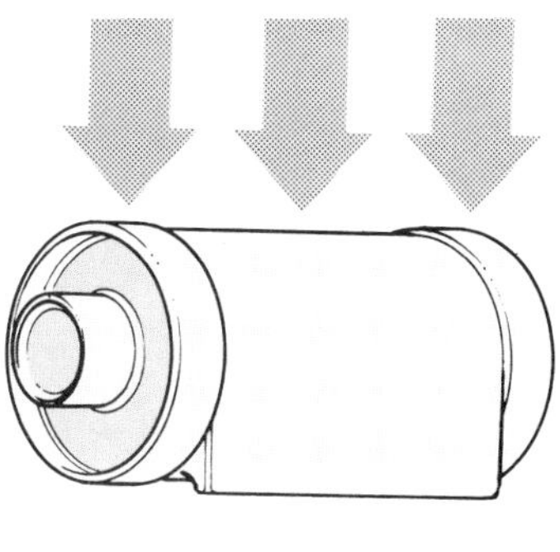

A prominent label is a useful precaution for camera cases travelling by air. If film is unavoidably subjected to X-ray examination, the direction the cassettes are facing may influence the amount of damage.

SUNLIGHT

Daylight is the richest and most varied illumination available for photography, as well as being the most common. One of the most important steps in learning photography is an appreciation of the role that lighting plays. The technical side of light and exposure is actually fairly straightforward, much more significant is the quality of the light – this can make or break a photograph. The more you know about the causes and effects of the many conditions of natural light, the better equipped you will be to use it.

The two basic factors that control the quality of daylight are the position of the sun in the sky and the atmospheric conditions, like cloud and haze, which diffuse it. The height of the sun above the horizon determines the brightness, and also the texture and contrast of surfaces. The colour temperature depends on this as well, but for black-and-white photography this is not a consideration. As it rises in the morning, the light passes through less atmosphere than when the sun is low, so that in the middle of a typically bright, clear day in summer in middle latitudes, the exposure on ISO125 film would need to be somewhere in the region of 1/125sec at f/16. This is the basis of a useful exposure principle for the occasions when your light meter has broken down or its batteries failed: for bright, sunny weather, use an exposure setting equivalent to 1/ISO film speed at f/16. With no clouds, this holds true between mid-morning and mid-afternoon in summer.

ABOVE Strong overhead sunlight produces deep shadows in photographs which can be highly unattractive in portraiture, but can add both depth and atmosphere to architectural pictures such as the one shown here.

ABOVE RIGHT The simplest solution to the problems of shadows in sunny conditions is to move your subjects into the shade, where the light is softer. Because you are working with black-and-white film, you have no worries about the slight colour cast that appears when using certain colour emulsions.

Natural Light Conditions

CONDITION	GENERAL FEATURES	EFFECT ON CONTRAST	EFFECT ON SHADOWS	FAVOURED SUBJECTS
High sun	Difficult to add character to a shot	Low with flat subjects, high with subjects that have pronounced relief	Tall and angular subjects cast deep shadows underneath	Subjects that are graphically strong in shape, tone or pattern, eg some modern architecture
Low sun	Great variety, depending on direction and weather; may be unpredictable	High towards sun, medium-low facing away	Strongest with sun to one side; least with sun behind camera	Most subjects suitable, particularly scenics
Twilight	Low light level only distinguishable when sky is clear	High towards light; low facing away	Shadows usually weak	Reflective subjects, eg automobiles
Haze	Enhances aerial perspective	Slightly weakens contrast	Slightly weakens shadows	Some landscapes, some portraits
Thin cloud	A mild diffuser for sunlight	Slightly weakens contrast	Slightly weakens shadows	Some portraits, some architecture
Scattered clouds	Dappled lighting over landscape, causing changing local exposure conditions	Slightly weakens contrast	Fills shadows slightly	Many landscapes
Storm	Unpredictable	Variable	Variable	Landscapes
Snowfall	Low light level; dappled, foggy appearance	Weakens contrast considerably	Weakens shadows considerably	Landscapes, natural & urban
Moonlight	Very weak light, but quality similar to sunlight	As sunlight	As sunlight	Many subjects that would look too familiar in daylight

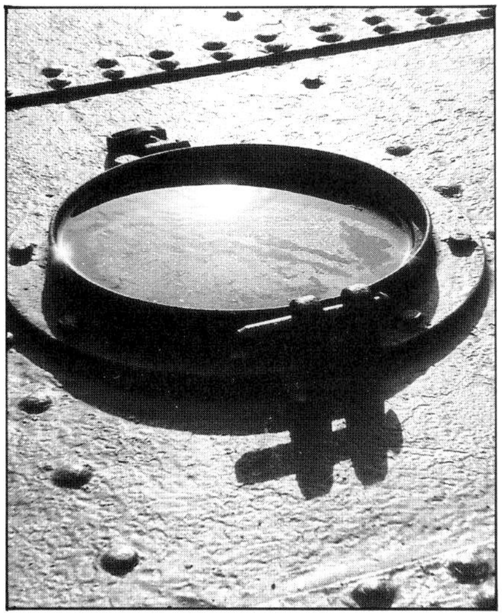

ABOVE Your ability to exploit texture will effect enormously your success with black-and-white photography. Low-angle sunlight can bring out the texture of materials beautifully.

The amount of textural detail depends on the angle of sunlight striking the surface, so for most flat landscapes a low sun gives the greatest impression of detail. Most landscapes are, in fact, mainly horizontal, and the beginning and end of the day are traditionally favoured times for outdoor photography. As the sun rises or sets, there is a period of an hour or two in which the brightness changes rapidly, as do the shadows cast by trees, rocks, mountains, buildings and so on. When shadows are nearly horizontal, subjects tend to be more dramatically and prominently lit.

There are even more possibilities for picture variety if you deliberately search for different camera angles when the sun is low. If you photograph into the sun, there are possibilities for strong, definite silhouettes, and of atmospheric flare from the sun itself. Cross-lighting, in which the sun is to one side of the view, gives a good modelling and textural effect, casting strong shadows and giving views with a reasonable range of contrast. Shooting with the sun can produce very clear, sharp views. The colour advantage of a low sun – rich, warm hues – does not apply in black-and-white photography, however.

The risk involved in shooting at these times of day is that if there are any clouds around, they are more likely to block the sun at this angle. In many places it is not safe to rely on a completely clear sunrise or sunset, but this uncertainty adds to the interest of location photography.

There may be an even closer choice between shooting at sunset and at sunrise – at least if there is a selection of views rather than one single subject. Dawn photography means getting up and into position early, and this may not be easy if you have to reach a viewpoint in darkness and anticipate exactly where the sun will rise. Only in the tropics does the sun rise and set almost vertically; elsewhere, it moves at a diagonal to the horizon, so that first light will not be in the same place as sunrise itself. In the northern hemisphere, sunrise is south of first light, and the higher the latitude the greater the distance between the two, as the sun rises at a shallower angle. In the southern hemisphere those directions are in reverse: sunrise is north of first light. In the late afternoon, all this is much simpler, as you can see for yourself the angle of the sun's descent.

RIGHT Shooting into a low, strong sun provides the opportunity for obtaining striking silhouettes. To achieve this, however, it is important to expose for the strongly lit background, and not the subject you wish to appear as a silhouette.

LEFT Although undeniably attractive, snow scenes photographed in strong sunlight can pose problems for built-in exposure meters. The meter may be fooled into under-exposure, reading the glare of the sunlight on the snow as the dominant lighting in the scene. Solutions include taking a separate exposure reading from the main subject – in this case the house – or taking an incident light reading with a hand-held meter.

As the sun moves higher, in the late morning, the quality of the light changes, and on a bright cloudless day the lighting effect can be quite stark – similar to that of an overhead spotlight. Shadows are cast underneath objects instead of to one side,and this is often unattractive. Portraits in particular suffer from the combined effect of high contrast and shadows that pool underneath the eyebrows and face. If you cannot avoid taking a portrait photograph under these conditions, it may be better to change the location, and position the sitter in a shaded setting. There are, with black-and-white film, no problems with colour temperature in doing this. There will be a considerable difference in the light level and contrast as you move from sun to shade, but this can be helped by choosing a setting close to a sunlit wall, or by using white card or cloth as a reflector.

ABOVE LEFT In general outdoor photography, look out for scenes in which there are already strong shapes and contrasting tones. They can produce graphic, hard images in conjunction with deep shadows and hard light.

TOP Although the warm hues of a setting sun are not available to the black and white photographer, it is possible to use flare when shooting into the sun to lend atmosphere.

ABOVE Even when working indoors, strong sunlight can be used to great advantage. Here, powerful rays have bleached out, giving the picture a 'classical' look.

In more general outdoor photography, look for scenes in which there are already strong shapes and contrasting tones. These, in combination with deep shadows and hard light, can produce hard, graphic images. Black-and-white materials also allow this effect to be exaggerated – a strong red filter will enhance both the dark tone of a blue sky and the shadows (which are illuminated by blue skylight), and a hard paper grade at the printing stage.

When the sun is in a medium-high position, it can be used for very high contrast images, either by shooting upwards from a low viewpoint, or by aiming towards the sun's reflection in water. Both cases can produce stark silhouettes.

The Difference a Filter Makes

BELOW Shooting into the sun always brings the risk of a bleached sky; but adjusting the exposure to compensate can lose all detail (bottom). The problem can be overcome to some extent by using a neutral graduated filter.

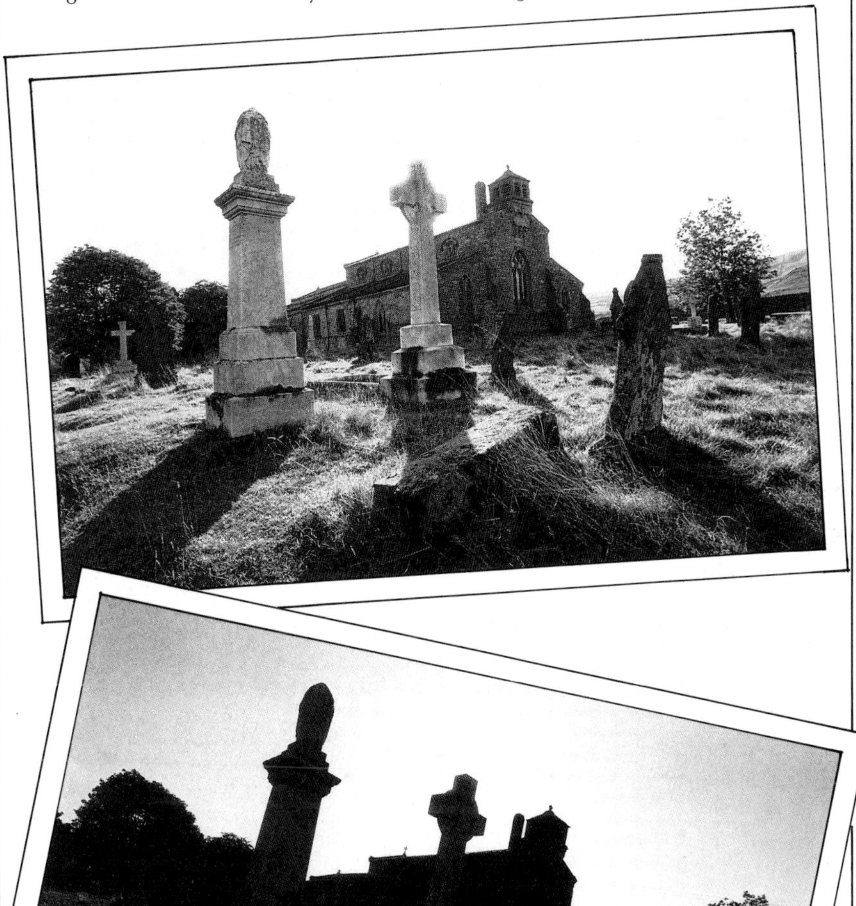

CLOUDS

Clouds alter the quality of sunlight by diffusing it, and also play an important role as components in a landscape. The extent to which they soften the light and reduce shadows depends on how thick the cloud cover is and on how high. So, a shroud of low, dense cloud diffuses light over the entire sky, to the extent that on a completely overcast day there are no outdoor shadows at all, and it may be impossible even to see the direction of the sun. Thin, high cloud, on the other hand, just takes the edge off shadows and highlights, and can help, for instance, in a very slight softening of a portrait.

As well as diffusing sunlight, cloud cover also reduces the amount, and this has an obvious effect on the exposure settings for the camera. As a rule of thumb, thin, high cloud can reduce the light level on the ground by up to one stop, a bright cloudy day has about a two-stop effect, moderately overcast about three stops, and strongly overcast (stormy) about four stops.

Although cloudy weather reduces local contrast by making the light more enveloping and weakening shadows, in a broad landscape it can actually in-

BELOW Ironically, cloudy weather can actually increase contrast between land and sky in a broad landscape. In these circumstances, a neutral graduated filter may be used to 'even up' the contrast.

crease the contrast between land and sky. There may be a modest difference in brightness between green fields and a blue sky, but it can reach up to five or six stops between the same landscape and a bright, overcast sky. In this kind of view, it can help either to use a neutral graduated filter or to give the sky extra exposure when making the print.

Clouds of different types and shapes can also make imposing parts of a landscape, and can even be dominant enough to make the main subject of a photograph. The most useful in this way, to be included as part of the composition, are those with distinct, precise shapes – fluffy cumulus, cirrus, or the anvil-shape of a thunderhead – and those with sharp tonal contrast.

In order to make the most of interesting clouds, it helps to use a wide-angle lens (to take in a broad sweep of the sky) and to place the horizon close to the bottom of the frame. Also, if the sun is more or less at right angles to the camera view, a polarizing filter will emphasise the contrast with the blue areas of the sky. The most useful filters of all for black-and-white photography, however, are yellow, orange and red, which darken the entire blue of the sky to differing degrees.

LEFT Clouds can be so striking that they demand to be made the dominant part of the composition. Best suited are clouds with strong, distinct shapes.

ABOVE Low cloud on hilltops can soften light beautifully, providing the photographer with the perfect opportunity to exploit the naturally strong texture of the landscape.

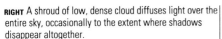

RIGHT A shroud of low, dense cloud diffuses light over the entire sky, occasionally to the extent where shadows disappear altogether.

DAYLIGHT INDOORS

Although the light source is the same, daylight in interiors is a rather different proposition for photography than it is outdoors. As it streams in through windows and doorways, it is a more localised kind of illumination, and it is also significantly weaker.

Despite artificial lighting, daylight is the most common illumination in most rooms. Nearly all interiors have windows, and in many cases a room appears at its most attractive in daylight. In fact, the interiors of some churches and most old buildings were designed to be seen and enjoyed by daylight, before adequate, powerful artificial lighting was possible.

Interiors are such static, predictable subjects that they lend themselves well to planning. In the kind of circumstances under which you might want to photograph a room, you are likely to be able to choose the time of day when you do it. So, the first decision to make is whether to take the picture in the daytime, by natural light, or whether to shoot later, using artificial light. You may find that the simplicity of daylight through windows best preserves a natural, authentic atmosphere.

The quality of daylight in interiors varies greatly, depending on where the windows are, how many there are, which way they face relative to the sun, and the size of the room. Generally, windows are set in one or two walls of a room only, so that the lighting direction tends to be horizontal, and the level falls off from one side to the other.

It is the relative proportions of windows and room size that control the contrast in an interior. A complete wall full of windows along a corridor can produce quite even illumination, whereas one small window in a square room

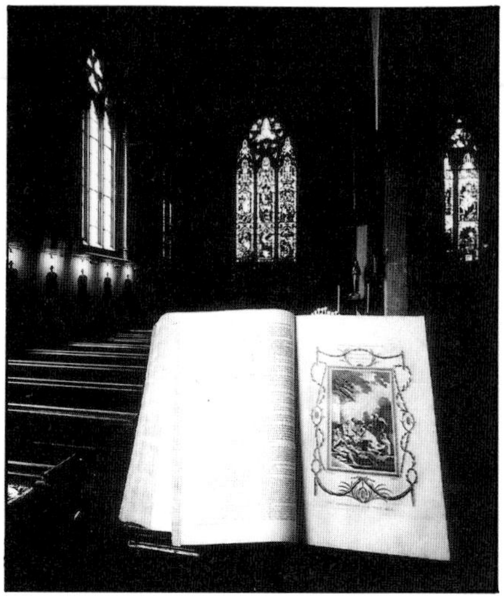

ABOVE In a scene where the window is to one side of the frame, it is usually best to counter-balance the uneven contrast by introducing light yourself. This may either be bounced flashlight, or even a reflector (such as a white card) to bounce the natural daylight back into the required area.

BELOW A perfect example of a situation where the use of any source of artificial lighting would totally ruin the atmosphere of the scene. Even the 'bleaching out' of the lighting pouring through the windows has enhanced, rather than detracted from, the image's charm.

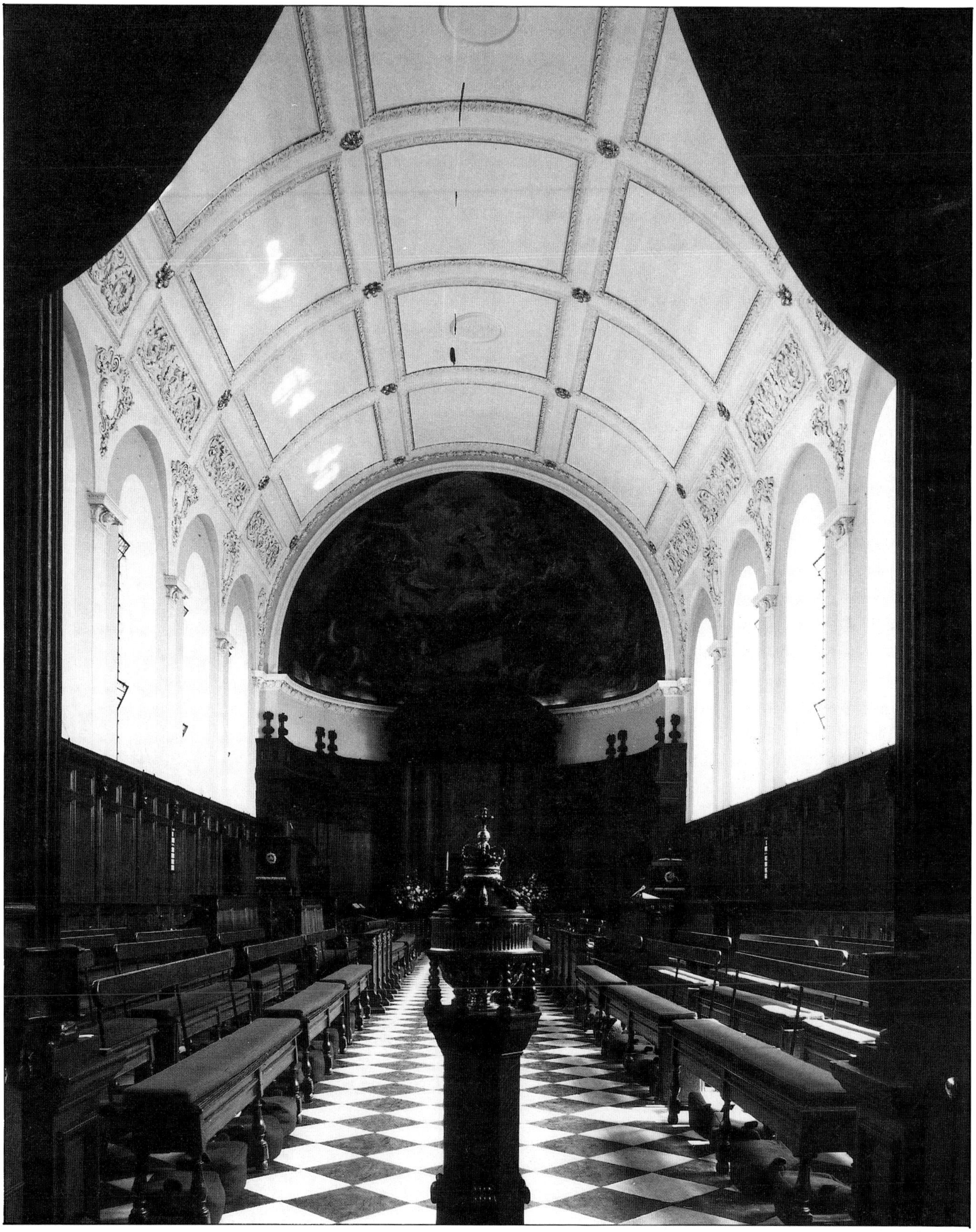

will create a high contrast range, with the level of light falling off very quickly. The window becomes the source of illumination rather than the sky or sun. If you are shooting across this contrast range, with the window on one side of the picture, it will usually be necessary to take some action to counterbalance the unevenness. Bouncing a photographic lamp off the opposite wall is one method Another is to shade the print when you are making the enlargement, giving more exposure to the darker side of the room.

ABOVE Since most churches were built well before the days of powerful artificial lights, the majority were designed to be enjoyed by natural daylight – hence the large windows.

PORTABLE FLASH

Most modern portable flash units are automatic in the sense that they contain some means of monitoring the light output and adjusting it according to the exposure that the picture needs. The simple way of doing this is for the flash to contain a light-sensitive cell that will measure the amount of light reflected back from the subject. Additional circuitry then quenches the duration of the flash as soon as a predetermined level of brightness has been reached. There are three important settings to be made when using this kind of automatic flash: the flash synchronisation speed on the camera, the film speed on the flash unit's calculator, and the lens aperture. The synchronisation speed varies between makes of camera: those with between-the-lens shutters will synchronise at any speed, while those with focal plane shutters have a limit, normally between 1/60 and 1/125sec, and sometimes simply marked as 'X'. The lens aperture can be set within the limits shown on the flash unit's calculator, and these depend on the distance of the subject.

A more sophisticated, and increasingly more popular, type of automatic flash is the dedicated unit. This is specifically designed for one model of camera, and often uses the camera's own through-the-lens metering system to control the flash exposure. A warning light indicates when the flash output has been insufficient.

The problem with using a flash directly from the camera is that the lighting effect tends to be flat, with only a thin edge of shadow, and that the exposure is only good for one distance. Usually, this results in underlit backgrounds, and occasionally, overexposed foregrounds. A standard answer to this is to bounce the light from the flash off the ceiling, or even off one wall. This softens and diffuses the light, as well as giving it an overhead direction. Many flash units have a swivelling head to allow just this, or the unit can be removed from the camera and aimed upwards. As the ceiling will absorb much of the light, a wider aperture is needed, by about 2 or 3 stops or even more if the ceiling is high or dark.

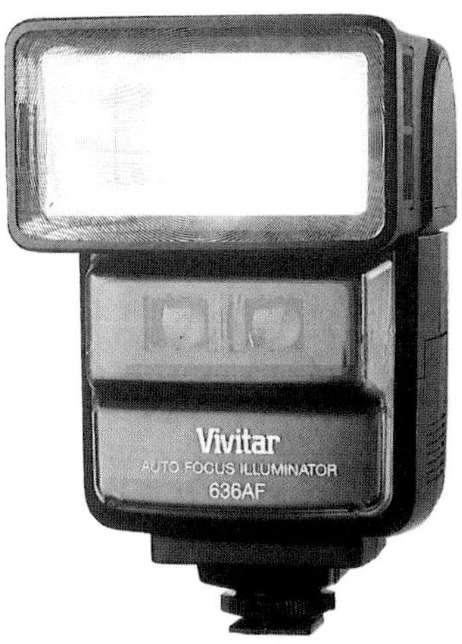

Flashguns are now available that act almost as 'seeing eye' dogs for autofocus cameras – they send out an infrared beam that measures the camera to subject distance, and instruct the SLR's AF system accordingly (top). Basic automatic flashguns (above) are fitted with a light-sensitive cell which 'kills' the flash light when a sufficient exposure has been made.

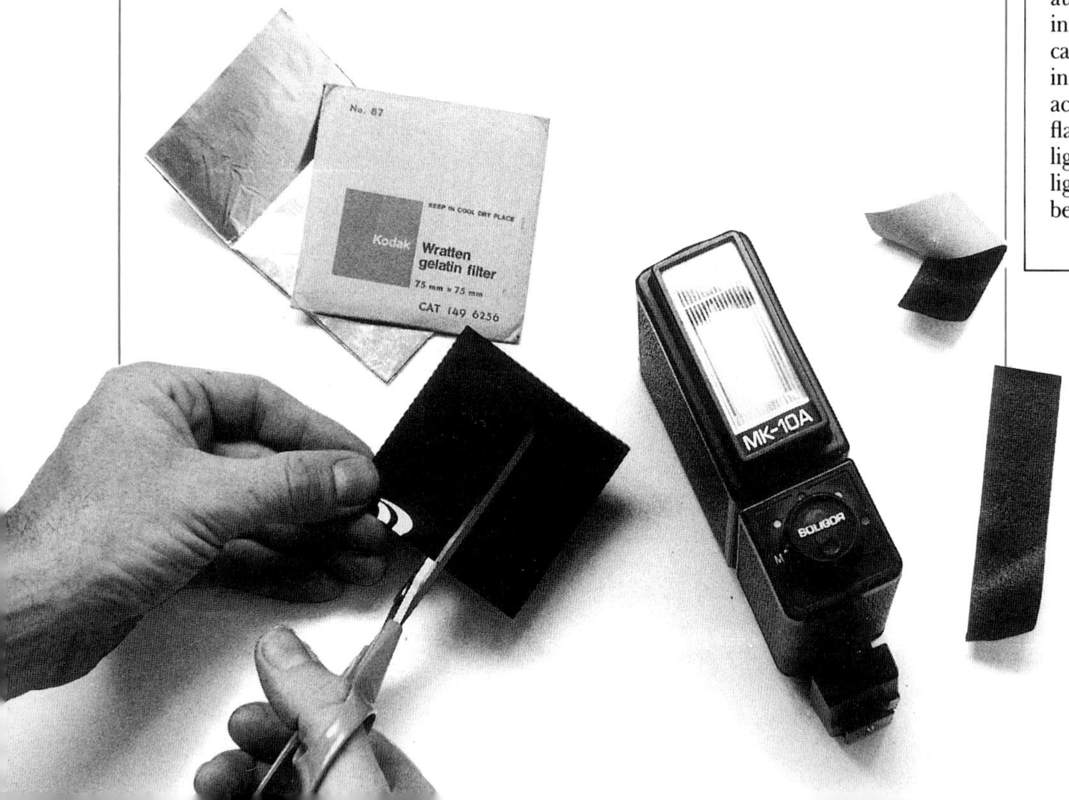

LEFT Gelatin filters are particularly useful when you want to colour or diffuse light from a portable flashgun, because they can be cut to shape and fitted over the flash head.

Bounce Flash

BELOW The only source of illumination in this scene is from the desk lamp, the result being that much of the facial detail has been lost.

LEFT However, light from a flashgun mounted off the camera can be bounced off a suitably reflective surface to regain the detail and give a natural, balanced look to the scene.

LEFT Portable units can be employed to great effect when backlighting still life subjects. In this case, the backdrop has diffused the light from the flashgun to overcome the problems of reflections within the bottle.

OTHER PHOTOGRAPHIC LIGHTS

Despite the convenience of portable flash, it gives little opportunity for creating attractive or interesting lighting – a typical unit is so small that it gives hard shadows when used directly and is too weak to give a useful light level if heavily diffused or reflected. For controlled indoor photography, different photographic lamps are needed, powered from a mains outlet.

There is a basic choice between electronic flash and tungsten lighting, and the decision about which to use depends on both cost and the type of photography intended. A typical mains-powered flash unit suitable for amateur use weighs several pounds and is a self-contained unit intended to be mounted on a lighting stand. More powerful systems have the flash heads separate from a power pack (principally capacitors and a control panel; but these are heavy, not so portable, and more expensive). Photographic tungsten lamps are, on the whole, lighter and simpler, a well as being cheaper. Both flash and tungsten lamps are designed to be used with attachments that control the diffusion and concentration of the light reaching the lens.

Flash freezes most movement and is relatively cool in operation – there is a low-wattage modelling lamp next to the flash tube to show what the lighting effect will be. The colour temperature is matched to the daylight and it can be used either in combination with existing daylight or in isolation, depending on the shutter speed. Guide numbers are not used for mains flash, as these units are hardly ever operated as naked lights; instead, the ratings are in joules (watt-seconds). A unit of 200 to 500 joules is sufficiently powerful for most indoor tasks with a 35mm camera.

Tungsten lighting is hot in use, but has two advantages. You can see exactly how the lighting will appear in the photograph, and there is no limit to the amount of light to which you can expose the film (it needs only a longer exposure time, whereas a flash unit must be triggered repeatedly, which can take even longer).

Two other kinds of equipment are needed for these lamps: supports and attachments for controlling the quality of the light. Lighting supports do not need to be quite as rigid as a camera tripod, but they must be fairly versatile. To make the most of a photographic lamp, you must be able to support it in a variety of positions, usually overhead. The basic support is a collapsible stand with tripod legs and an adjustable central column. For holding a light directly overhead, however, use a boom arm, ceiling fitting, or a crossbar supported beween two stands. The position of the lamp is often critical.

BELOW RIGHT The light from powerful electronic flash heads can be softened by bouncing it into an umbrella. The softening effect makes this technique particularly suitable for portraiture.
BELOW, MIDDLE A rondo light, or 'softbox', has the effect of diffusing light, spreading it over a relatively large area in the process. Suspending a softbox above a still life set is a common technique, giving as it does the gentle lighting so vital to this type of work.
BELOW Although hot in use – and therefore usually unpopular with models – tungsten lighting enables the photographer to see exactly how a scene will look in the finished picture.

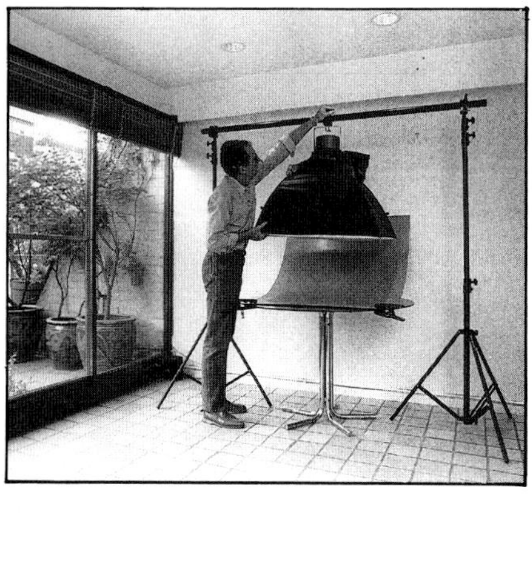

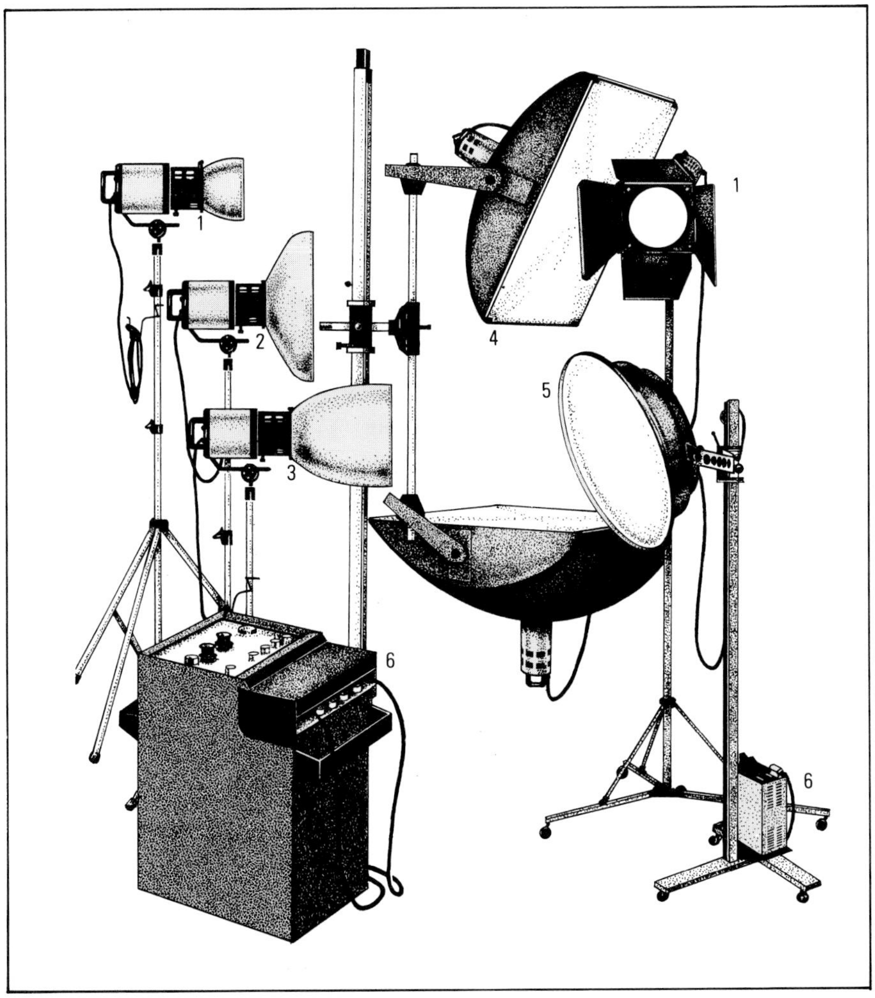

ABOVE AND LEFT Good lighting is essential for photography – a typical set of equipment includes a standard reflector (**1**), narrow angle reflector (**2**), soft light reflector (**3**), a hazy light (**4**), a rondo light (**5**) and the power pack (**6**). The spotlighting effect in the picture (top) gives sharp dense shadows, while in the high key shot (above) there are no deep shadows and the tones are from the light end of the scale.

The quality of the light depends on what you place in front of the lamp. As we saw earlier bouncing the light off a bright surface has an immediate softening and broadening effect, but there is no need to rely on the way a room is decorated. Portable diffusers can be bought or made, and include collapsible umbrellas (the inner linings can be white, silver, or even coloured, such as gold), sheets of white card or paper attached to stands, and large styrofoam/polystyrene sheets.

Diffusion gives a similar effect to most of these reflectors, but works in a different way. A translucent material is held in front of the light, which is aimed towards the subject you are photographing rather than away from it. Umbrellas of a different kind, with a translucent fabric, can be used in this way, as can tracing paper, thin white cloth stretched on a frame, opalescent plastic, or specially constructed boxes known as area lights. Diffusing a lamp rather than reflecting its light usually allows a smaller aperture setting.

Sometimes, instead of broadening the light and making shadows softer, a more concentrated spotlight effect is needed. The best attachment for this is a lens, but a cheaper alternative is a cone-like fitting known as a snoot, or even a sheet of black paper rolled into a tube.

Finally, the light can be shaded and directed, by using flaps attached to the lamp housing (known as barn doors), and by pieces of black card attached to stands and placed appropriately.

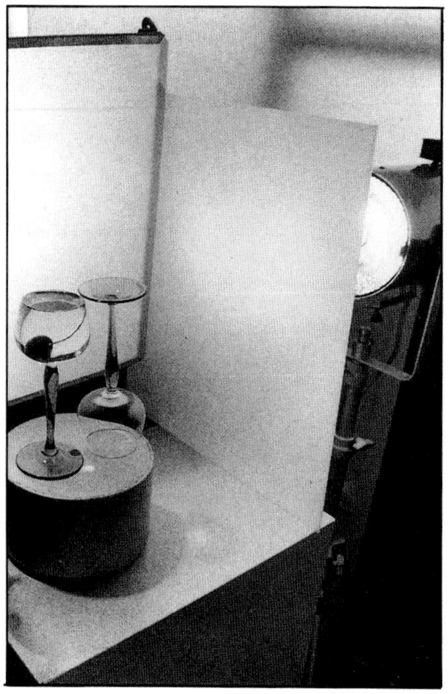

ABOVE A simple but remarkably effective lighting arrangement for use in the studio; note how the single light source is diffused with the use of a screen, guaranteeing that the results will not be harsh.

Equipment for Indoor Lighting

1 Electronic flashgun plus battery pack.
2 Re-chargeable power pack for . . .
3 . . . A ringflash, for use in macro photography.
4 Electronic flashhead.
5 Reflector hood for flash.
6 An umbrella, for reflecting flashlight.
7 Flashhead with reflector hood attached.
8 Hand-held light meter.
9 Snoot, for directing studio lighting.
10 Booms and stands, for supporting flash heads.
11 A flashgun plus re-chargeable battery pack.
12 An SLR plus bracket-mounted flashgun.
13 Lens filter holder.

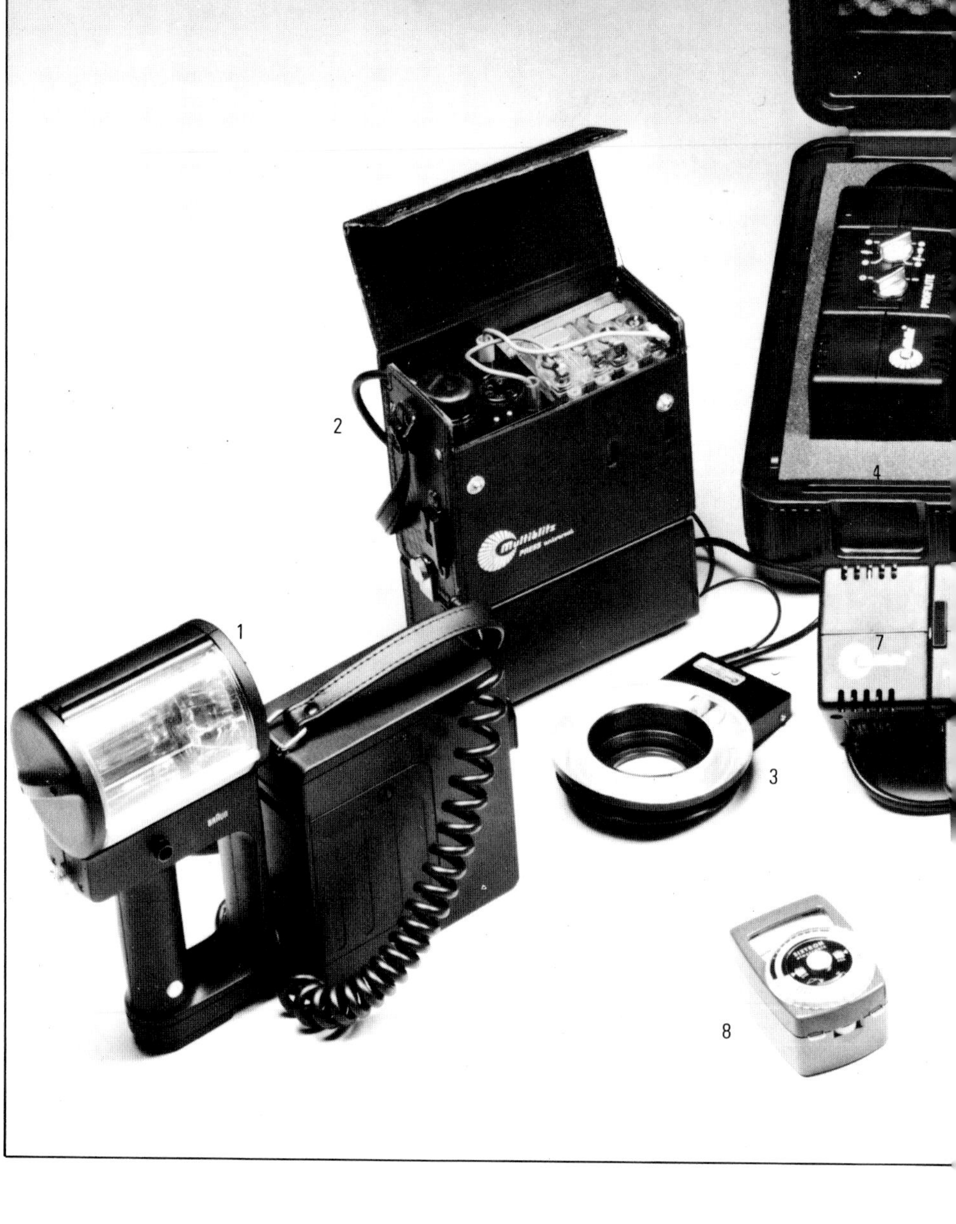

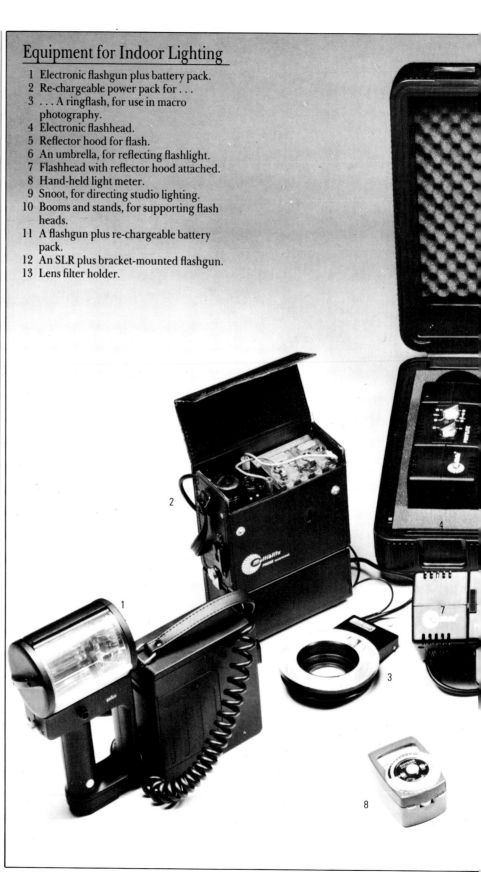

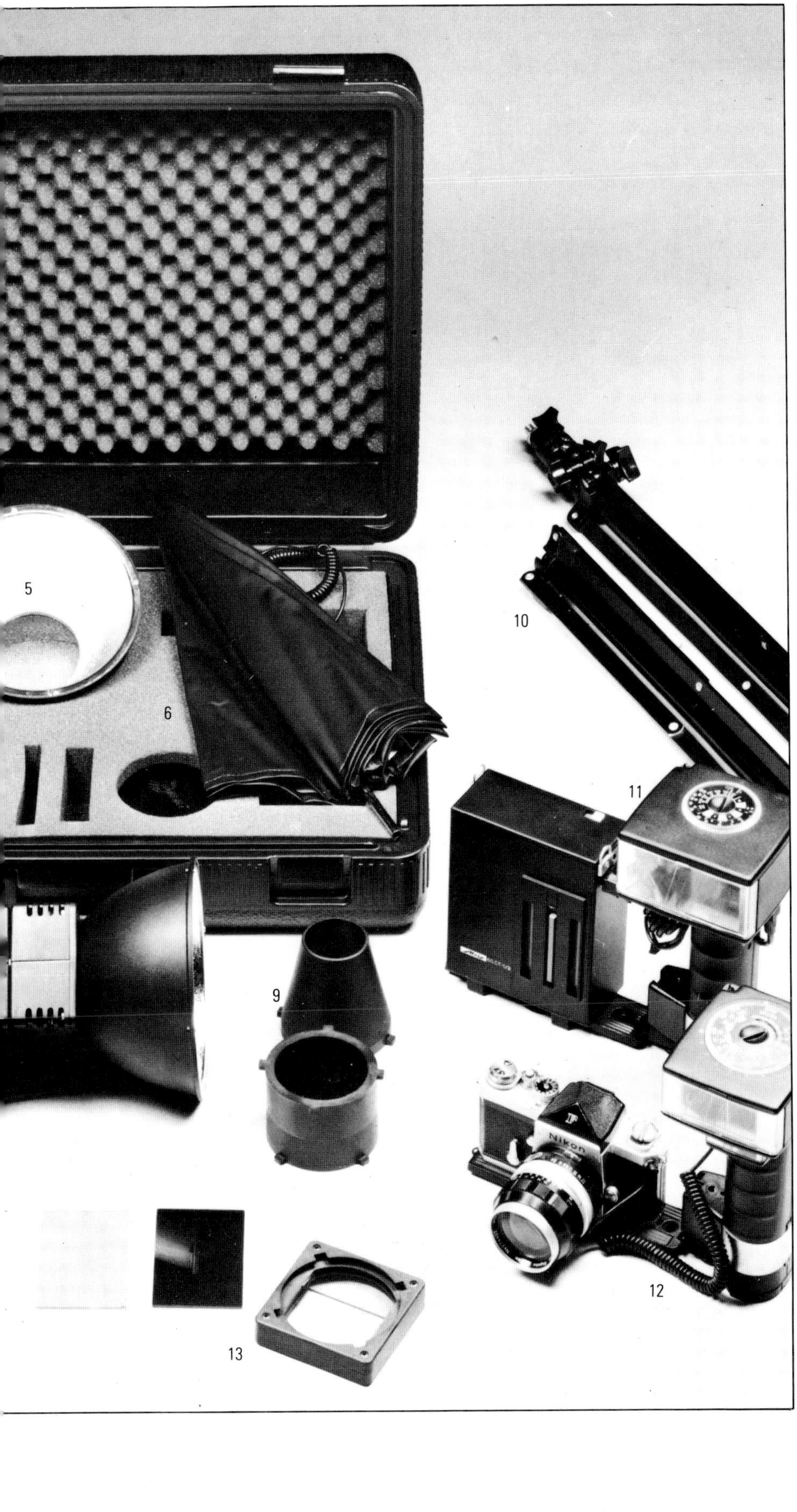

TOP A typical studio set-up for still life work; a softbox – literally an electronic flashlight contained within a box, one side of which is covered with a diffusing material – is suspended above the set to give gentle lighting. The white card is arranged as shown to give 'seamless' results.

ABOVE A great shot – but note that diffused lighting had to be used, or else the reflective subject would give harsh results.

EXISTING LIGHTS

Existing light is generally taken to mean illumination that is artificial but not intended for photography. As we have already seen, film, lens aperture and shutter speed are all built around a normal standard that is geared to outdoor daylight, and even though this varies over a range of several stops, it is still an entire level apart from the much weaker lighting found in interiors and, of course, at night.

There are particular problems in photographing by existing light. Principally, they are a low level of illumination, which limits the kind of photography that is possible, and high contrast caused by the unevenness. The colour balance of existing artificial light is also often unusual, but fortunately this is no concern for black-and-white photography.

FOCUSING AND FRAMING

The first obvious problem at night and in dark interiors is that it is simply not easy to see what you are doing. As far as the camera controls are concerned, some makes have built-in illumination – either LEDs or a small lamp that is activated by a special button to light up the now more usual LCD. In any case, however, a pocket torch or flashlight is an essential piece of equipment.

Composing and focusing the image is difficult with a single lens reflex, as the mirror and focusing screen together absorb a considerable amount of light. This is not so obvious in bright daylight, but in low light conditions the image is likely to fall below a workable level. If you can replace the focusing screen easily, a full microprism grid is an answer: microprisms absorb less light than the ground area of the glass. Otherwise, you may have to rely on a distance scale engraved on the lens. Rangefinder cameras score heavily in low lighting: the straight-through optical viewfinder is almost as bright as a direct view. One tip: in either case, use points of light for focusing. Wide-angle lenses have greater depth of field and so need less critical focusing; equally, however, they are expected to give sharply focused images, so that gross focusing errors are particularly obvious.

BELOW Shooting in low light levels can bring focusing problems. One solution is to use points of light in a scene, such as the lamps here, to focus upon.

OPPOSITE Another solution to the focusing problem is to exploit the added depth of field inherent in a wide-angle lens; because so much of the scene will remain sharp, you have fewer worries about focus being spot on.

EXPOSURE

It may not always be possible to make a useful exposure measurement from the position of the camera, with any kind of meter. A typical problem situation is when the subject of interest is relatively small in the frame, well lit but surrounded by a dark setting. This, for instance, would apply to a floodlit building in the middle of a town, seen from a distance.

The first thing, therefore, is to be quite clear about what part of the scene you need to measure. The advice given earlier about exposure readings applies to low light levels as well as those in full daylight. Bearing this in mind, there may still be a problem in registering any reading at all with the meter. Most meters have a fairly modest limit in the order of a few seconds of exposure time, and although they will do for most conditions, it is likely to be insufficient if you are using slow film at night.

Nevertheless, there is a solution: change the film speed rating just for the reading. If, for instance, you are using ISO50 film and cannot get a reading even at full aperture and with the slowest shutter speed on the dial, simply turn the film speed selector up until a reading appears. Note the new ISO setting and increase the exposure accordingly. In this example, say that the speed selector needed to be turned as far as ISO200 before a correct reading was shown; this is 2 stops faster than the film speed in use, so the exposure time would have to be multiplied by four. Remember to reset the shutter speed selector back to the ISO value of the film afterwards. There is also likely to be some reciprocity law failure at speeds of several seconds – use the table below for compensation.

STEADYING THE CAMERA

In low light, slow shutter speeds are normal. To an extent, you can improve your ability to shoot at slow speeds without extra support by practice and by learning how to hold a camera correctly – keep your elbows into your body, breathe out slowly and squeeze the shutter release gently. Even so, always look for any nearby support at a convenient height, such as a low wall or railings. A wide-angle lens allows slower shutter speeds than a telephoto, because things in the viewfinder are magnified less. As a realistic goal, aim to be able to shoot without camera shake at 1/30sec with a standard 50mm lens, 1/60sec with a 100mm lens, 1/125sec with a 200mm, and so on. Nevertheless, as you cannot rely on finding an adequate resting place exactly where you need it, if you are setting out to take night-time pictures, carry a tripod and use a cable release.

BELOW This table suggests exposure adjustments for correcting reciprocity effects with Kodak general-purpose black-and-white films.

Exposure and Development Compensation for Reciprocity Characteristics — KODAK Black-and-White Films

KODAK FILM	Exposure Time in Seconds	1/1000	1/100	1/10	1	10	100
Tri-X Pan Plux-X Pan* Verichrome Pan Panatomic-X*	Increase Lens Opening by	None	None	None	+1 stop	+2 stops	+3 stops
	Or use Corrected Exposure Time in Seconds	No Change	No Change	No'Change	2	50	1200
Recording 2475	Increase Lens Opening by	None	None	None	+⅔ stop	+1⅓ stops	+2⅔ stops
Technical Pan 2415	Increase Lens Opening by	None	None	None	None	+⅔ stops	+1⅓ stops
	Or use Corrected Exposure Time in Seconds	No Change	No Change	No Change	No Change	—	—

* Information also applies to KODAK PLUS-X Pan Professional and PANATOMIC-X Professional Films.

Basic Camera Handling

With a 35mm SLR in its normal horizontal shooting position, the most stable hold is to support the base of the camera on the heel of the left hand, gripping the right side of the body with the right hand. Press the camera against the face, and keep elbows tucked well in. Wrapping the strap tightly around one wrist also helps to steady the camera. For vertical shooting, a 35mm SLR can be supported either way, depending on personal preference. With a motor-drive fitted, the camera can usually be supported entirely by a right-hand grip.

Where conditions allow, and especially when using a telephoto lens – which is particularly prone to the effects of camera shake – make use of all available means of support. These including squatting, kneeling, using the camera bag as a rest, and nearby walls.

CHOOSING THE EXPOSURE

One of the most important, and basic, skills in photography is controlling the quantity of light that reaches the film. In particular, it is essential to be able to record exactly the right level of light to achieve the effect you want. This is the basis of choosing an exposure setting: converting one particular brightness level (in the scene) into a certain range of tones in the photograph.

Nearly all modern cameras have built-in through-the-lens exposure meters, some of them quite sophisticated in the way they analyse the light. Also, the trend towards automation continues and increasingly camera meters measure the light and select the exposure controls without any need for the photographer to become closely involved. Nevertheless, setting the exposure is not entirely a mechanical process – or at least, should not be. The idea of 'correct' exposure applies only to recording as many of the tones of the scene as possible, and not to any aesthetic quality. Having full control over the image means exercizing judgement. This in turn means being able to override whatever meter you use. It is not good practice to rely so completely on an automatic meter that you lose touch with the practicalities of exposure.

Exposure meters, of whatever kind, measure the quantity of light, and then indicate an exposure setting that will reproduce this as an average tone. Most meters average all the tones in the scene to a common value. In a typical through-the-lens meter, the top of the frame is almost ignored, because in an outdoor setting, most people compose the view to include some sky at the top. This is known as 'weighting' the meter pattern.

In a normal scene, this way of judging the exposure setting works well most of the time, but there are likely to be problems if the distribution of tones is in any way out of the ordinary. For instance, a small bright object against a dark background will turn out to be overexposed with this method, and a large bright background, such as with a backlit portrait, will over-influence the meter to cause under-exposure. An averaging meter gives every scene the same treatment: in black-and-white photography it shows the settings needed to produce a mid-grey, whether the subject is grey, black or white. Ultimately, therefore, you must judge the scene for yourself, and decide how much darker or lighter than an average grey you want it to appear in the photograph.

Fortunately most film in most situations will accept a margin of error. This is called exposure latitude, and black-and-white films have more latitude than colour. To an extent, unsatisfactory exposure can be corrected during printing, by using a different paper grade and altering the enlarger exposure. Nevertheless, you should always be within one stop of an accurate exposure.

LEFT If there is a suspicion that your camera's built-in exposure meter may be fooled by a scene, and no hand-held meter is available, resort to bracketing. This technique involves taking one shot at the meter's suggested exposure, then two or three on either side of the meter's ideal. In this case, the photographer has shot the ideal (opposite, top), then two more frames have then been shot, increasing the exposure by a half-stop for each. The process has finally been repeated, only this time the photographer has under-exposed.

RIGHT Although black and white negative film is far more tolerant of over-and under-exposure than colour slide film, it is still vital that you aim for the most accurate exposure possible. Compare the ideally exposed picture in this series with those both under-and over-exposed around it.

Taking Readings

The four basic methods of using a hand-held meter:
1. With the reflected-light method, the meter is pointed directly towards the subject to measure the light.
2. With contrasty subjects, it is a good idea to take readings from the brightest and darkest areas of the subject and then make a compromise between them.
3. An 18% gray card, which has average reflectance, can be used as a substitute for the subject.
4. An incident-light reading measures only the light falling on the subject. A translucent plastic cover is fitted to the meter.

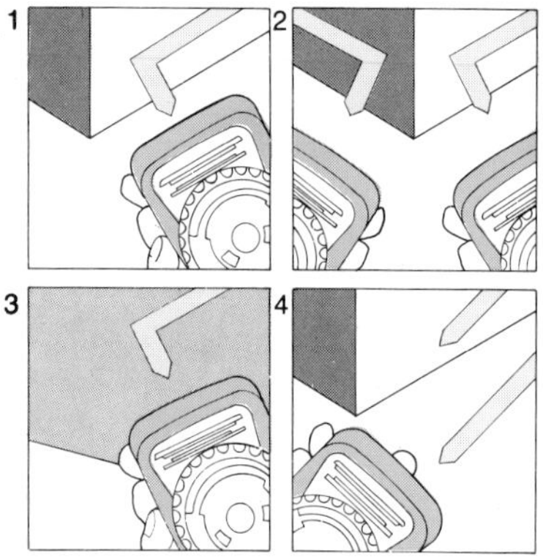

CHOOSING THE EXPOSURE

There are three basic methods of measuring light and exposure, although only two are possible with a camera's through-the-lens meter. They are: reflected light readings, incident light readings, and substitute readings. Each has its advantages in certain conditions. Incident light readings can only be made with a hand-held meter fitted with a specially diffused receptor, but they are so valuable in some situations that most serious photographers carry one.

REFLECTED LIGHT READINGS

These can be made either with the camera's through-the-lens system or a hand-held meter pointed directly at the scene. The meter measures the light reflected from surfaces, and so a combination of the intensity of the light itself and the inherent darkness or brightness of objects. It is ideal for uncomplicated lighting conditions in which there are no really great differences in tone across the image. However, if there are strong shadows and bright highlights, an average reflected light reading may not give an accurate exposure for what is important in the picture. Instead, it is normal to take two readings, one from a shadow and the other from a bright area, and set the exposure halfway between. For such two-part readings, a spotmeter is very useful; with the camera's built-in meter, you should either approach the subject more closely to make the reading, or change temporarily to a longer focus lens.

Another alternative, useful if the important part of the picture is very small and either brighter or darker than its surroundings, is to limit the area that you measure. Here again, use a spotmeter, move closer, or switch to a lens with a narrower angle of view.

INCIDENT LIGHT READINGS

The second method of measuring exposure is to ignore how bright or dark the subject is, and record only the strength of the light falling on it. This is the principle of the incident light reading, which is made with a hand-held meter that has a milky white plastic dome fitted over the light sensor (this is removable so that the meter can be used for incident or reflected light readings).

The technique is to hold the meter in the same position as the subject – or at least in the same lighting, if the subject is not conveniently accessible – pointing the receptor towards the camera. The great value of this method is that the setting is not confused by dark or light subjects.

SUBSTITUTE READINGS

By measuring the light reflected from a surface that you are already familiar with, you can make reflected light readings that are not influenced by the subject. The most accurate substitute is an average grey, and a card made for this purpose can be bought from photo dealers.

BELOW Grey scales are commonly used to take substitute readings, whereby a measurement is taken of light being reflected from a surface that you are familiar with. The reflected light reading is not, therefore, influenced by the subject.

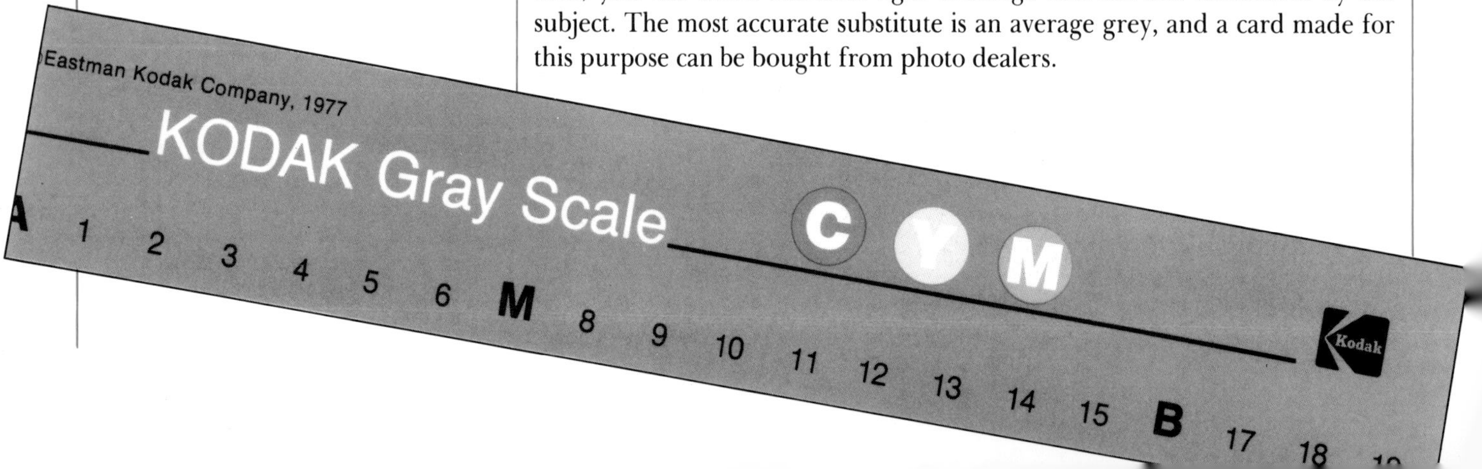

Shading the Meter

When using a hand-held meter outdoors, shade the meter with your hand so that the reading is not overly influenced by the sky.

TOP LEFT High contrast subjects may require a modification to the standard reflected light reading technique. Instead of a single reading, two should be taken; one from the highlights, and one from the shadow. The correct exposure should fall half-way between.

LEFT Unlike the above example low contrast scenes usually only need a single reflected light reading. This can be done either with a hand-held meter pointed directly at the scene, or with the camera's TTL light meter.

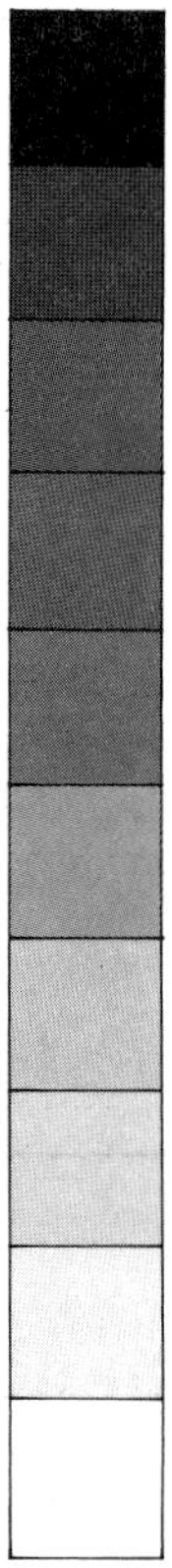

The Zones

0 Solid black; the same as the film rebate (edges).
I Nearly black; just recognizably different from Zone 0.
II The first hint of texture but nothing recognizable.
III Textured shadow; the first zone to show recognizable shadow detail.
IV Average shadow value on Caucasian skin, landscape foliage and buildings.
V Middle grey; 18% grey test card; the 'pivot' value; light foliage; dark skin.
VI Caucasian skin (36% reflectance); textured light grey; shadow on snow.
VII Light skin; bright areas with texture, such as snow in low sunlight.
VIII Highest zone with any texture.
IX Pure untextured white; little difference between this and unexposed paper.

ABOVE A typical scene with a contrast range of approximately seven stops. Fortunately, a typical black-and-white negative coupled with normal Grade 2 printing paper can handle this, although it is important to place the zones correctly.

THE ZONE SYSTEM

For really fine control over exposure, entire systems have been invented at different times. The most famous of these is the Zone System, used by one of the greatest black-and-white photographers, Ansel Adams. This is certainly a more complicated approach to exposure than is usual, but it does make it possible for the photographer to be in complete control of the tonal values in the image. It takes time, and so is best suited to the photography of static scenes, such as landscapes and architectural subjects.

The Zone System assigns all the levels of brightness in a scene, and all tonal values, to a scale of ten steps. Each of these steps is exactly one stop different from the next, and the scale goes from pure black to pure white. As you can see from the strip (left), Zone 0 is solid black, Zone V in the middle is an average mid-grey, and Zone IX is pure white. By assigning the important tones in the scene to the appropriate zones, it is relatively easy, once you are experienced, to see how the contrast range of the subject fits that of the negative and the print.

In many photographic situations, contrast is something of a problem, or at least demands careful attention. A typical scene has a contrast range of about seven stops, and so covers seven zones. A normal black-and-white negative, together with a typical Grade 2 printing paper (this is the normal grade); can handle this range, but it is important to place the zones correctly.

One of the most important zones is III – textured shadow. This is the value at which dark details can just be seen, and is generally thought of as being a tone that should be preserved in the print. This zone is 2 stops darker than average, and a typical procedure would be to measure it with an exposure meter and then adjust the settings on the camera to 2 stops less than the one indicated.

Comparing the brightness levels in the scene with the 10-step scale shows which parts, if any, will fall outside the film's brightness range. Treat a medium-speed black-and-white negative film, developed and printed normally, as having a range of seven stops.

RIGHT Zone III, textured shadow, is one of the most important, since it is the value at which dark details can just be seen. Its dominance in this portrait made it vital that it should be preserved in the finished print.

How the Zone System works

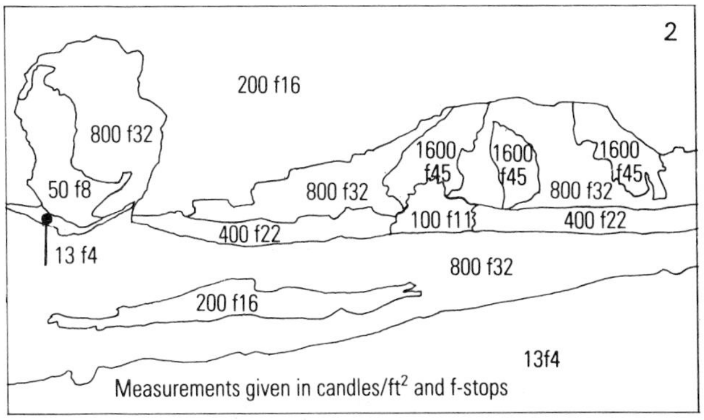

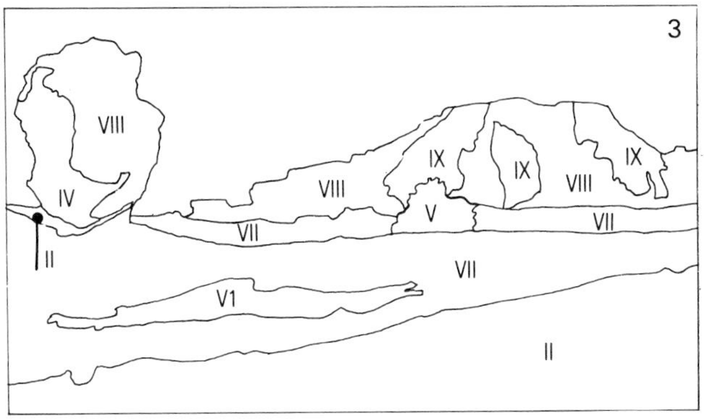

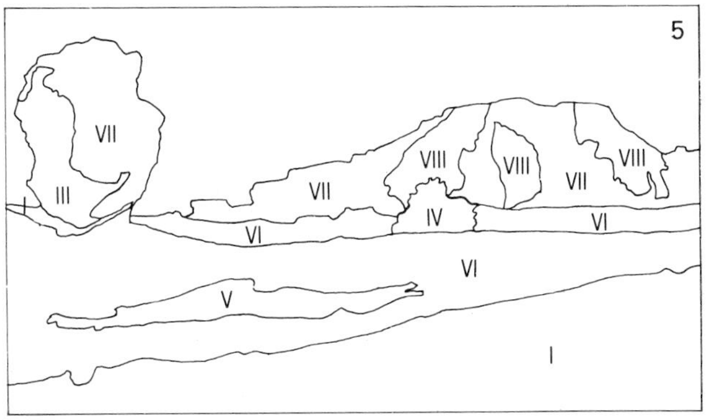

This sunlit scene covers many brightness values – in other words, it has a high contrast range.

Because we are discussing the tonal reproduction that a photograph offers, the original subject is represented here as an illustration (1).

Stage 1: Using the measuring methods described already, we can make a precise, objective record of the brightness levels in this original scene.

Different exposure meters record their information in different ways. The next picture (2) shows the scene measured in candles-per-square-foot $(c/ft)^2$, a universal measurement, but not one normally used by photographers, and also in f stops – by assuming a film speed of 100 ASA and a shutter speed of 1/125 sec.

Stage 2: At this stage the photographer has to decide subjectively what are the important areas of the scene. Because Zone III ("textured shadow") is defined as the darkest shadow area in which detail is actually wanted, it is quite common to use this as the key zone. In this example (3), however, the immediate foreground is critical, for while it does not cover any significantly interesting detail to merit Zone III, it should have at least a hint of texture in the final print. So, as a first experiment, by placing the foreground in Zone II, everything else will fall in its own particular zone. This creates a problem with this scene, because the areas of the sandstone cliffs and rocks inevitably fall in Zone IX, which means that their texture will not register (4). In other words, the contrast range in the subject is too great, a common problem.

Stage 3: Unless something is done to alter the high contrast, either in the subject, the negative or the print, we will have to compromise by sacrificing detail at one end of the scale. In this example, it would certainly be better to sacrifice the foreground shadow detail (5). By moving everything down one zone, the foreground becomes nearly black (Zone I), but the cliff highlights become a satisfactory Zone VIII (6).

This completes the visualization, and all that remains is to make the exposure. We have calculated how the final print will look before even taking the shot – the essence of the Zone System's use.

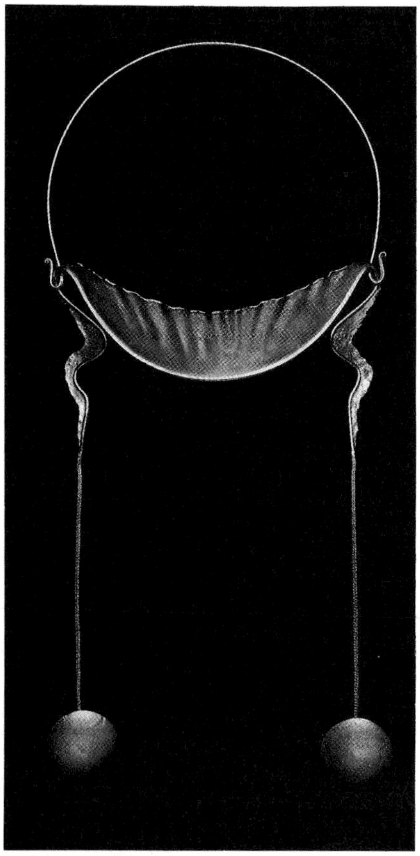

ABOVE To some, it is just a negative; to others, particularly photographers who enjoy printing, it is a store of endless possibilities. As many black and white enthusiasts maintain, a single negative is the start of a million different prints.

RIGHT A Calotype taken in 1848 by Henry Fox Talbot, the inventor of the technique. The image is a positive taken from a negative, which allows multiple prints; a fundamental of photography today.

OPPOSITE Since a black and white picture can never be truly realistic, it has the advantage of being a means of expression which can elicit particular emotional responses rather than simply a recorder of reflected light. Put simply, it is *the* craftsman's tool.

A CRAFTSMAN'S FILM

Black-and-white film occupies a special, and unusual, place in photography. If you think about it dispassionately, it might seem that black-and-white is simply a poor relation of realistic colour, and that there is no very good reason for continuing with a medium that is outdated.

Certainly no-one invented black-and-white film and paper because they offered anything more than colour emulsions. In the nineteenth century, photography began with black-and-white because it was the only thing possible. There is little doubt that, had the chemistry been within the scope of the then current technology, colour would have been there from the start, and black-and-white imagery would in all probability never have emerged. A monochrome picture is relatively simple – indeed, the starting point for colour film also, which is composed of three layers of black-and-white emulsion with the addition of coloured dyes.

Nevertheless, black-and-white so dominated the early decades of photography that it became established, and acquired its own traditions. When colour arrived, it inevitably replaced the monochrome image for most of the photography market, but black-and-white had already made enough of a mark that it became, as it now remains, the medium of the craftsman.

What black-and-white offers is a kind of refinement. Without hues, the image is thrown back on fewer graphic qualities, and these must be used more carefully to make successful pictures. Even more important is the matter of realism. Colour film has the possibility of reproducing, in two dimensions, every visual aspect of an occasion or view. So many people expect no more of it than this: a record of things as faithful to the original as possible.

Black-and-white suffers from no such prosaic expectations. It can never be completely realistic, and this gives it the singular advantage of being able to be treated as a means of expression rather than just a documentary record.

RIGHT Like straight diagonals, curved lines convey a sense of movement to the viewer, although it is tempered with a feeling of smooth, gentle progress, in this case across the scene from left to right.

BELOW A prime example of how a graphic eye can seek out an attractive picture with little raw material. Here, the photographer has noticed the strong diagonal formed by the row of beach huts, and framed the scene to make the most of this.

LINE

In an image that must work with a single scale from dark to light, the basic graphic elements have a special importance. These are the components of all images: lines, shapes, forms, texture and the tonal range. Powerful black-and-white photography usually makes conscious use of one or more of these. The subject of a photograph may well be the most important and memorable part of the picture, but how you, the photographer, treat it graphically can make an enormous difference. It is even possible to make compelling images out of their design alone, with objects that are themselves of little interest.

The most basic of these elements is the line. It can be long, short, straight, curved, in different directions and of different thicknesses. Lines can separate the parts of a picture or join them, and they often have an irresistible tendency to pull the viewer's eye along, leading it from one area of the frame to another. While there is no pure, single line in nature (everything has some thickness and substance), they abound in images as edges and as connections between strings and rows of objects. The painted line on a road, the edge of a building, the horizon, and the stem of a tall plant are all obvious lines; the eye and brain, however, also make up lines from only a few clues. A row of soldiers on parade is interpreted as a line, but so is the direction in which a moving object travels. Even the direction in which a person looks can be interpreted as a kind of line.

Lines can have an understated psychological effect, giving a sense of movement or an impression of mood. For instance, horizontal lines tend to produce feelings of stability and solidity, while vertical lines have rather more energy. Diagonals have the most sense of movement, instability and dynamism. Curves also have some of the diagonal's movement, but temper it with a feeling of smooth gentle progression. Much of this stems from the experiences that certain lines conjure up. Gravity has much to do with the different sensations from horizontal and vertical lines; flat surfaces are bases, and supports for objects.

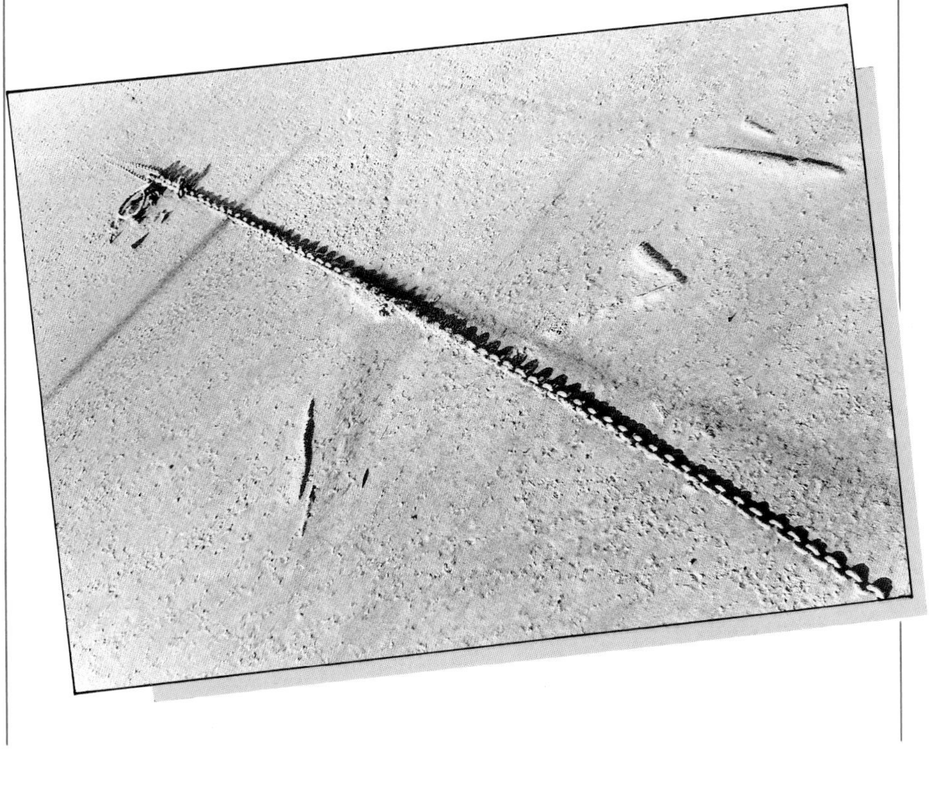

ABOVE Exploiting lines can be a matter of being aware of potential. Here, the converging guitar necks draw the eye, and tipping the guitars towards the viewer has given the picture further punch.

BELOW LEFT Although sometimes not immediately apparent, line has an understated psychological effect. In this case, a simple diagonal cutting across the frame has lent a dynamism to what is a very basic photograph. In effect, line is the subject.

SHAPE

If lines are the basic element in the construction of an image, the next level up is a combination of lines that encloses a particular shape. An enclosing set of lines is called, appropriately enough, an outline, and it is this that creates shape. Shapes exist in two dimensions, on flat images rather than in the real world: they are the projections of things, lacking volume. In other words, they are constructed by the eye, and are important as recognition symbols in human vision. How effective they are can be seen in the ease with which we can understand a complicated object from only a simple silhouette – the profile of a person's head, for example.

In fact, not only is a silhouette the most exact and pure version of a shape – it is also one that black-and-white photography is particularly well suited to recording. Silhouettes are the product of high contrast due to back-lighting: typical examples include a tree on the brow of a hill against a dusk sky, or a figure standing in an open doorway seen from inside. Anything that heightens the contrast beween the subject and its bright background will enhance the effect, and there are more opportunities for this with black-and-white emulsions than with colour. The exposure is important – not so full that it records details within the silhouette – but even more can be done in the printing, by choosing a 'hard', contrasty grade of paper. Indeed, a perfect silhouette is always possible by using lith film; this can be used for the original photography, or later, to make a conversion of a more normally toned original.

To a lesser degree, shapes in black-and-white photography are thrown into prominence by any distinct tonal contrast. Without resorting to any darkroom manipulation, shapes can be made the focus of the image by deliberately seeking out the juxtaposition of light and dark. The less convoluted the outline, the more the sense of shape comes through.

Because shape in photography is the projection of an object onto a flat surface, the orientation and the camera viewpoint alter our perception of things. A spoked wheel seen flat-on is perfectly obvious, but end-on is hardly recognizable. This is not necessarily a problem, but if you intend to use shape as an aid to recognition in a picture, give some thought to which angle gives the clearest view.

RIGHT Any distinct tonal contrast in black and white photography throws shapes into prominence. Shapes can be made the focus of the image in the darkroom by deliberately seeking out the juxtaposition of dark and light.

ABOVE The two-dimensional nature of shapes in black and white photography means that you must adjust the way you view a three-dimensional world.

BELOW Even if a certain amount of detail can be seen in the negative, it is possible to enhance the silhouette effect by choosing a hard, contrasty paper at the printing stage.

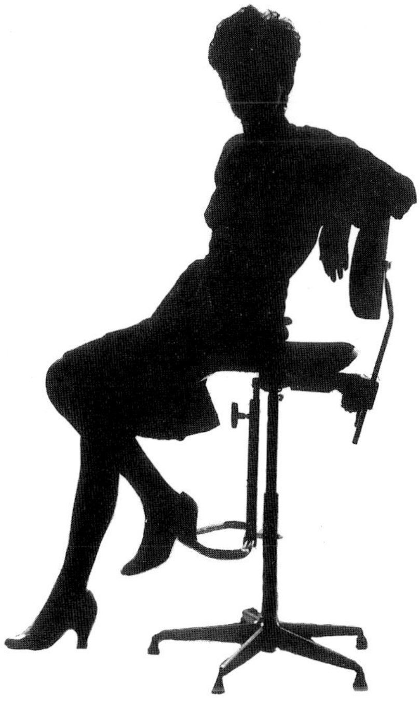

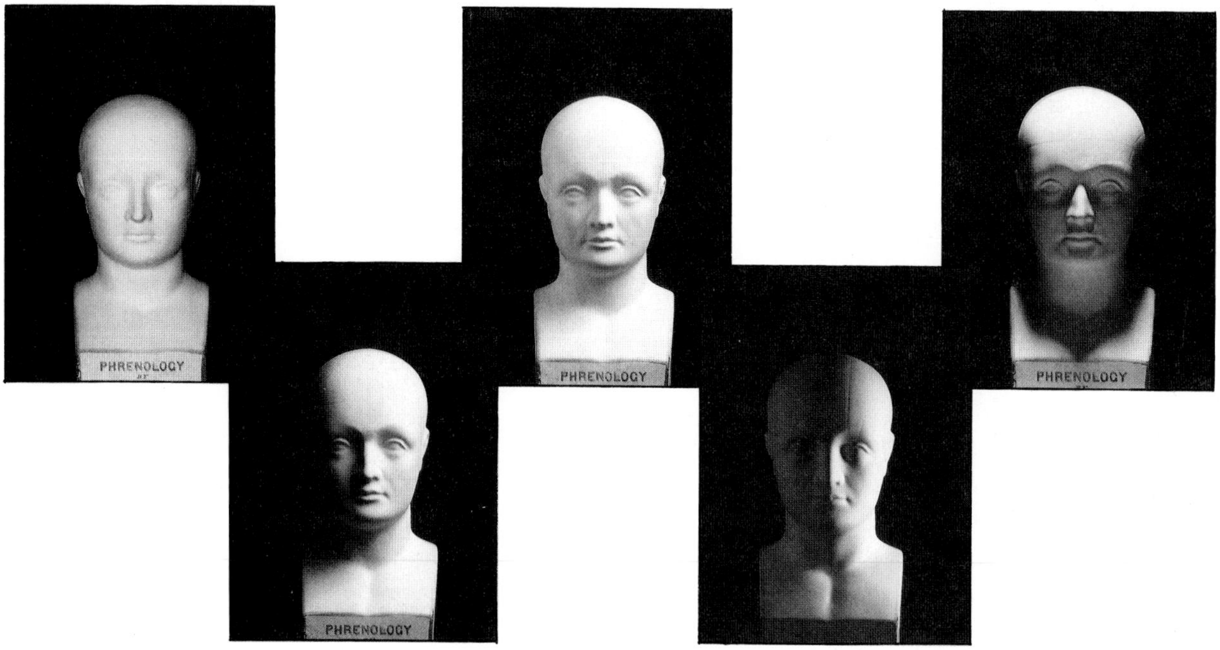

ABOVE Proof positive that our eyes use shading as the most vital clue to form. Simply adjusting the position of the light in relation to the subject alters the perception of it completely. From fairly straightforward frontal lighting (top row, left) to top lighting (top row, right), from hard lighting from a single side (bottom row, left and right) to off-centre top lighting with a reflector (top row, centre), basic adjustments to a lighting arrangement can drastically alter the impression given by an image.

FORM

From shapes, one step further towards realism is form. This is the volume of an object, a sense of its three-dimensionality. Whereas it takes our familiarity and imagination to construct the depth and tangibility of an object from its shape alone, a photograph with a good sense of form makes this obvious by the distribution of tones.

In fact, a number of techniques combine to convey form, not the least of which is lighting. Still-life photographers, whose success depends largely on their ability to design lighting sets that are appropriate to particular objects, are among those most concerned with form. The approach of an experienced professional to a new subject for a study is first a careful examination to appreciate the kind of volume it has. To take objects at random, a fist, a coin and a delicate orchid have clearly different forms, and each needs a different lighting approach.

While form should not necessarily dictate the lighting treatment, it is essentially an attribute of realism. A strong sense of form normally goes hand in hand with clear, unambiguous representation. Techniques that aid abstraction, such as those to enhance a silhouette, work against form. As you can see from these examples, the class of lighting that usually best conveys depth and volume is that of moderately diffused side-lighting. With this, the gradation of tones across the surface of an object produces relatively gentle transition from highlight to shadow.

Our eyes use shading as a clue to the form of something. As long as the light source seems to be in a conventional position, the brain calculates from the play of tones across the surface what the projections and depressions are. A useful experiment is to take one object, one light, and make minor adjustments to the position of the light and to the level of diffusion, making a series of comparative photographs.

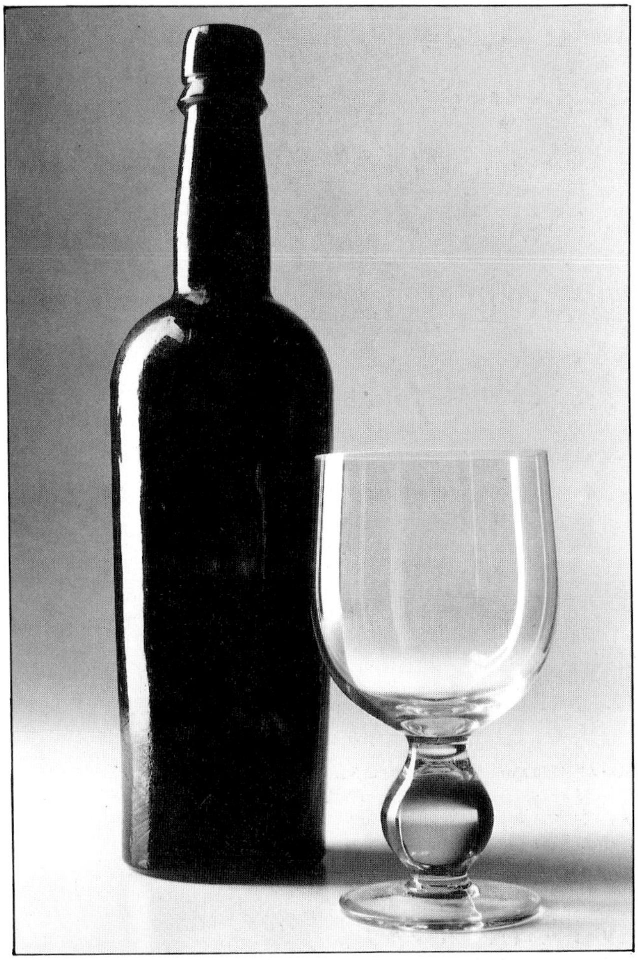

ABOVE Still life photographers, whose success depends upon their ability to match lighting sets to subjects, are particularly concerned with form.

ABOVE LEFT Diffused sidelighting is ideal for conveying a sense of form, producing as it does relatively gentle transitions from highlight to shadow.

LEFT Using light to accentuate prominent features in the subject, like the larger flat facets of this mineral, can enhance form.

TEXTURE

Texture is the surface quality of an object and, like form, is distinctly three-dimensional. While it can be used in making abstract images, its principal value in photography is as an aid to conveying realism. In many kinds of shot, one of the aims is to get across to the viewer as close a representation as possible – to make it almost tangible. If the texture comes across strongly, this helps the sense of realism enormously.

Food photography, for example, needs all possible help to convey taste (itself not a visual quality in any way). Texture, because it is related to taste, nearly always plays an important part, and photographers who specialize in food normally take great pains with the lighting to reproduce tactile sensations – the crumbling roughness of pastry, or the glaze on a roast ham.

Lighting is the key to texture just as much as it is to form, although the techniques are different. Textures also vary enormously, not only from rough to smooth, but in individual character: the leather binding of a book and the surface of smooth sand, for example, share a similar degree of roughness, but are immediately distinguishable in a photograph.

For fine texture, the strongest impression of relief comes from very low, direct illumination that just skims the surface. Revealing texture in black-and-white is largely a matter of using the lighting to throw shadows. Fine texture needs hard-edged shadows to be distinct, and for this the light source needs to be naked. Look at the effect of bright sunlight when it just grazes a wall.

The same hard, raking light applied to a rough, knobbly surface may sometimes throw too much of the texture into shadow. If the indentations are deep, a more diffused light is likely to give a better sense. Also, texture does not always need to be taken to the maximum in photography. There are occasions when a less definite texture is desirable. In portraiture, for example, while a lined, weather-beaten face may make a striking character study, a portrait that is supposed to flatter the sitter is not likely to get a good reception if it throws wrinkles into prominence! In fashion and beauty photography, much of the lighting technique is concerned with softening skin texture by diffusion, shadow fill, and a lighting direction that is fairly frontal. Even the finest skin contains some blemishes; these are a texture that is usually less than welcome.

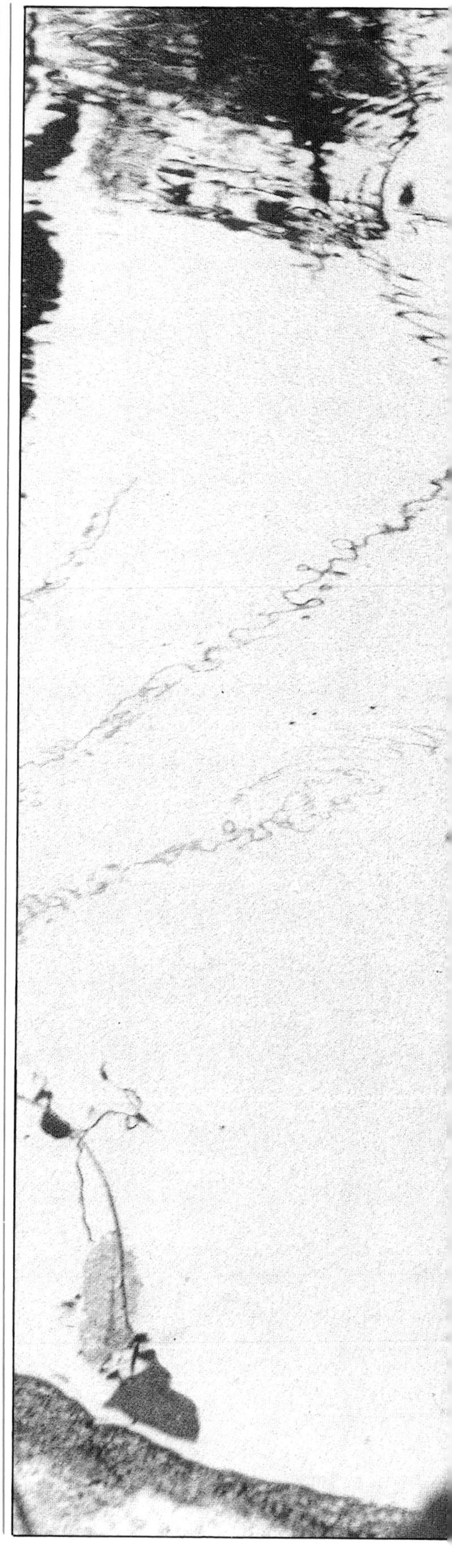

RIGHT Raking light applied to a knobbly, rough surface can throw too much of the subject's texture into deep shadow, ruining the picture in the process. As in the case of this photo of a crocodile, it's best to wait until the light becomes more diffused, either by waiting for cloud or placing the subject in the shade.

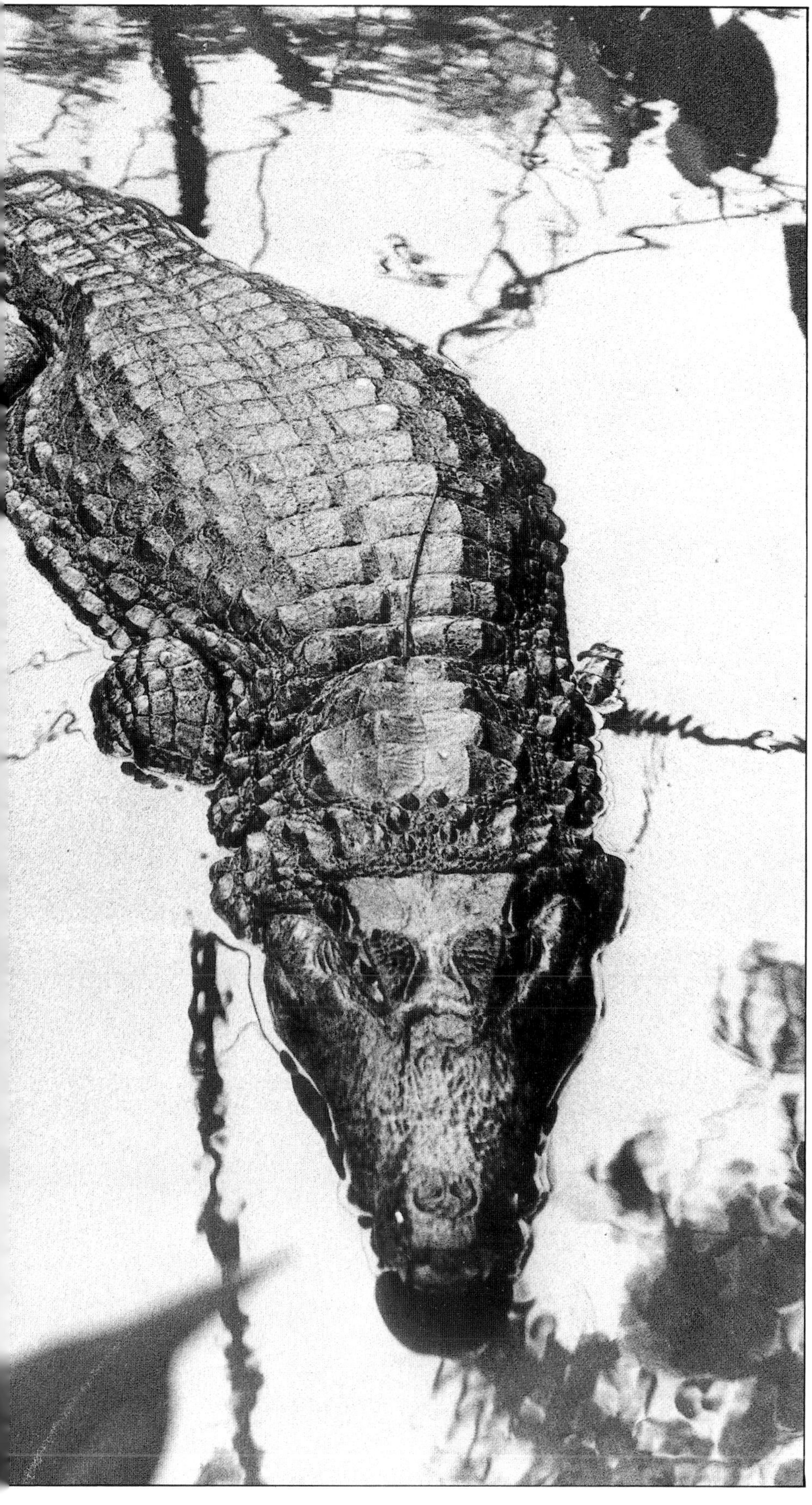

ABOVE For a still life such as this, where texture is all important, it may be necessary to adjust the image's contrast at the printing stage to make the most of the picture. In this case, the contrast has been lowered in the finished print.

COLOURS INTO TONES

Because black-and-white film converts from real life into tones, these tones can be altered, more or less at will. All that is needed is a set of coloured filters – coloured more strongly than the correction and light balancing filters common to colour photography. By choosing an appropriate filter, you can selectively manipulate the various shades of grey in an image. This freedom to experiment with the tonal relationships in a scene is one of black-and-white photography's strong appeals.

Often, however, a filter may be needed simply to compensate for a deficiency in the way that a monochrome film records light. The shade of grey in which a particular colour records depends on both the intensity of the light and on the spectral sensitivity of the film. Red, for instance, records paler than normal on the negative because film is relatively insensitive to it; in the print, therefore, it appears dark. At the other end of the spectrum, blue, to which film is more sensitive than our eyes are, exposes strongly onto film, and so appears pale in the print.

RIGHT Filters allow the photographer to manipulate toner and compensate for the deficiencies in the way that monochrome film records light. Because film is more sensitive to blue light than red, then red, yellow or orange filters can be used to compensate. Neutral density filters (top left and centre) can reduce the overall exposure – if, for example, you are using fast film on a bright day. Graduated filters (centre right) are excellent for 'deepening' a sky while not affecting the tones below the horizon.

Filtering Colours into Tones

Each of the four distinct colours in this still life – green, red, blue and yellow – are susceptible to alteration by filters. With no filter used, the over-sensitivity of normal black-and-white film to blue and its under-sensitivity to red give pale tones to the cigarette packet and a too-dark version of the red Dutch cheese on the left of the picture. A yellow filter lightens the yellow cheese and darkens the blue design on the cigarette packet. An orange filter performs a similar function to the yellow, but more strongly. A red filter dramatically lightens the red cheese and darkens the blue packet. A blue filter turns the yellow cheese almost black. A green filter lightens the tone of the apple, but makes the red cheese appear black.

No filter

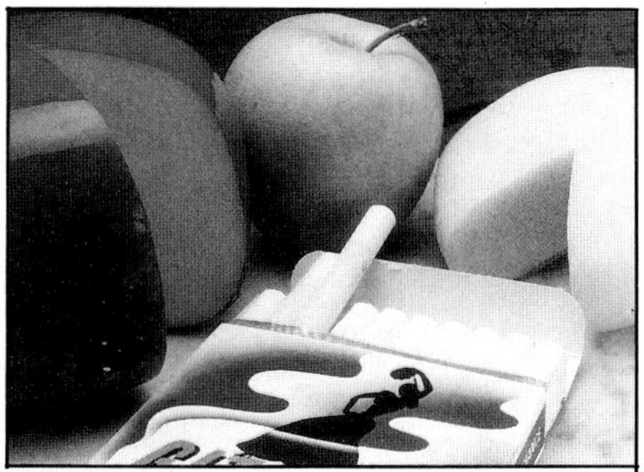

Wratten 8 yellow

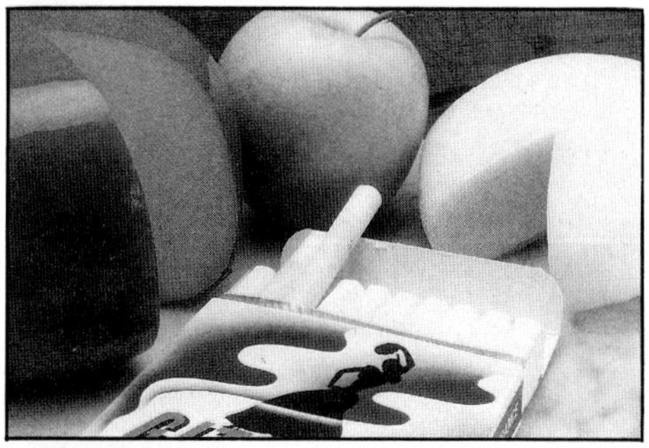

Wratten 16 orange

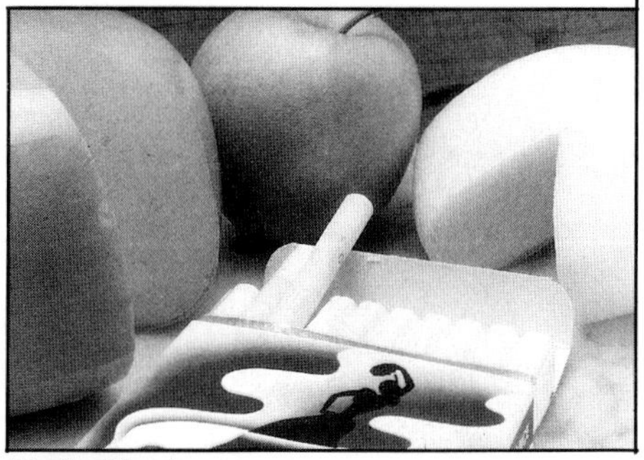

Wratten 25 red

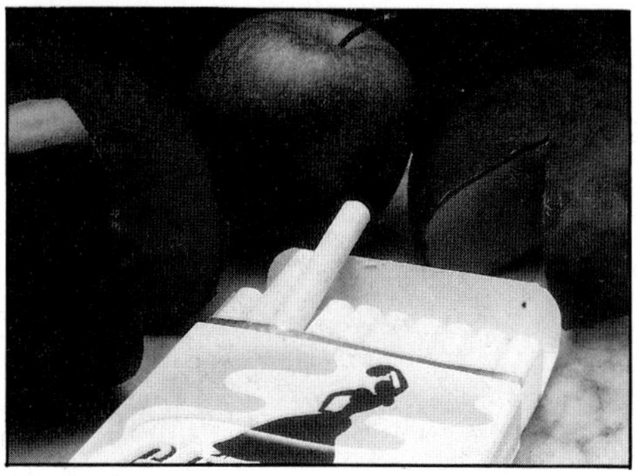

Wratten 47 blue

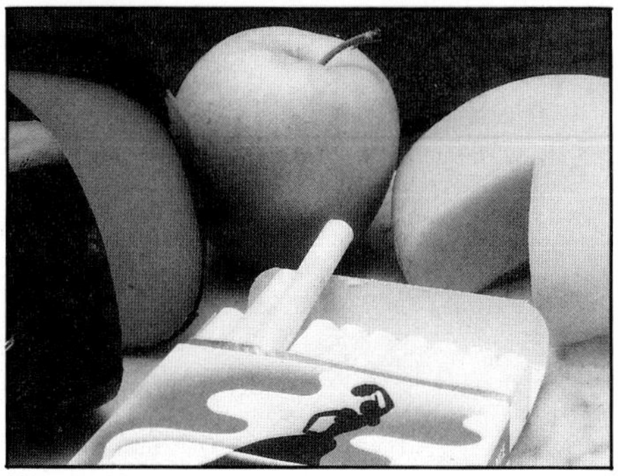

Wratten 58 green

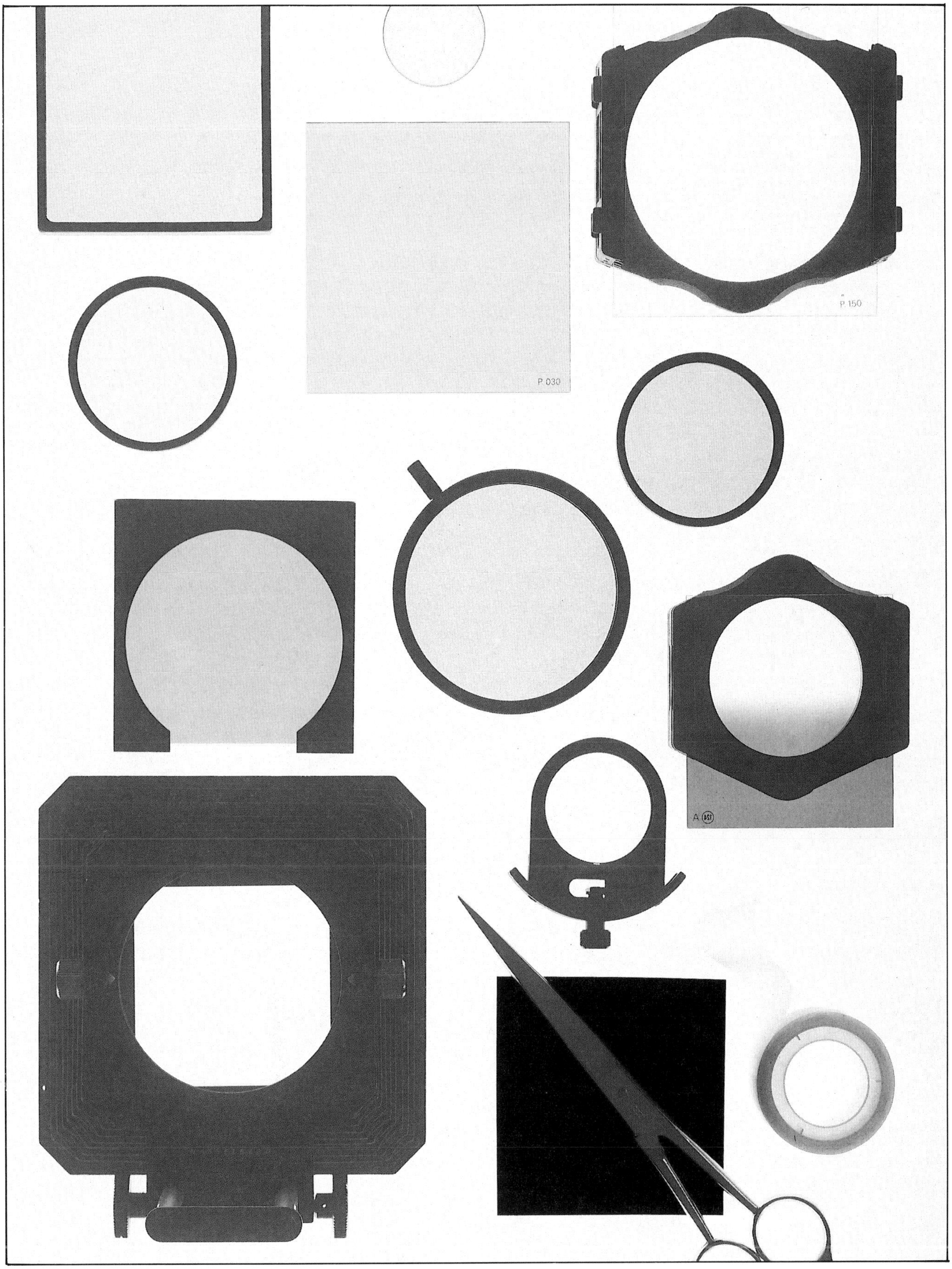
P 150
P 030

No filter

Blue filter

Red filter

Yellow filter

The best, and by far the simplest, way of appreciating the dramatic changes that can be made to a black and white photo is to put theory to the test. Compare the sky in the unfiltered picture (top) with the lacklustre sky in the picture taken using a blue filter (second from top). Then note how using a yellow filter (second from above) has restored the blue to an acceptable strength. Finally, compare the unfiltered picture with the red filtered shot (above); the extremely dark sky produced by using a red filter may not be to everybody's taste.

These are the two major differences in sensitivity to colour between film and the human eye, and as the eye is the final arbiter, the uncorrected photographic version may look unnatural. How important, or even how noticeable, this is depends on the familiarity of the scene. For instance, it is not likely to matter whether a red telephone looks almost black in a photograph – for all that the viewer knows, it might well be black. A tomato, however, is a different matter, as is red lipstick: we expect these to be a certain tone. Equally, we think of a blue sky as having a substantial tone, that ought in black-and-white to be a shade of grey something between medium and medium-pale. However, an uncorrected shot that includes the sky will show it as almost white because film is over-sensitive to this colour.

The principle of using coloured filters to control the tone is quite straightforward. Whatever the colour of the filter, it will pass its own wavelength but block out the remainder. As an example, a strong red filter, such as a Wratten 25, will allow the red components of light through, but hold back most of the blues and greens; this is something you can check just by holding it to your eye. Now, most scenes, and certainly most natural ones, are made up of combinations of colours, and there are surprisingly few pure, unadulterated hues. For most of a picture, therefore, this red filter will make only small differences. The red telephone mentioned above, however, will look very pale indeed – almost white – while anything green will appear virtually black. The rule is: use a filter of the same hue if you want to lighten the tone of a colour, but use a filter of a complementary hue to darken it. Complementary colours are the opposites; if mixed, they would cancel each other out. Place a red filter over a green one, for instance, and the result will be neutral and almost opaque.

The best-known tone control in black-and-white photography is to darken a blue sky, and for this a yellow, orange or even red filter is used. A yellow filter gives an approximately normal rendering – to the eye, that is. The reasons for darkening the sky are only partly to do with film's over-sensitivity to blue; in a typical landscape composition, a pale and featureless sky lets the attention drift off towards the top. A darker tone above often helps to pull the eye back down into the frame.

The strength of the filter's effect depends not only on the density of the filter, but also on the colour purity in the subject. Blue sky is strongly affected, but many colours in nature give disappointing results. For example, you might expect a green filter to make vegetation appear quite pale. In practice, particularly with overall views of trees, the effect is weak, because most such greens are in fact degraded with browns, yellows, and other colours.

In addition to using filtration to correct tonal values, it can also be used to manipulate them to suit your own tastes. Green and red of about the same intensity are immediately different in a coloured view (they are almost opposites), but in monochrome they may look very similar, and juxtaposed be difficult to tell apart. Using a filter of either colour will increase tonal separation.

As a filter passes less light through to the film, the exposure usually needs to be increased. The best guide to this is the filter factor; do not always rely on the camera's through-the-lens meter, as this has a colour sensitivity that is rather different to that of the eye.

Filter Checklist for Black-and-White Film

All the filters below, except the polarizer, are available in either glass or gelatin. As the glass thickness can distort, high optical quality is important in a filter, and this is expensive. Gelatin filters, on the other hand, are too thin to affect the optics of a lens, but must be handled carefully to avoid marking.

FILTER (KODAK WRATTEN NO.)	EFFECT	USE	FILTER FACTOR*	ADDITIONAL F STOPS*
Yellow 8	Absorbs UV and some blue	Darkens blue sky to an acceptably normal tone, accentuating clouds. Lightens foliage	2×	1
Deep yellow (18)	Absorbs UV and most of the blue	Similar to yellow but with a more pronounced effect. Also darkens blue water and lightens yellow subjects, such as some flowers	4×	2
Red (25)	Absorbs UV, blue and green	Turns blue sky and water very dark, increases contrast and deepens shadows. Cuts haze and lightens red objects. In portraits, lightens lips and skin blemishes	8×	3
Green (58)	Absorbs UV, blue and red	Lightens foliage and slightly darkens sky. Makes red objects darker and deepens skin tone in portraits	8×	3
Blue (47)	Absorbs red, yellow and green	Lightens blue subjects, increases haze in landscapes	6×	2½
Neutral density	Absorbs all colours in equal proportions	Reduces exposure, enabling a slower shutter speed or wider aperture to be used	Various	Depends on which filter factor
Polarizing	Controls reflections and darkens blue skies at right angles to the sun	Can eliminate reflections when photographing still water and windows. Darkens blue skies under some conditions.	2.5×	1½
Ultra-violet	Absorbs ultra-violet	Cuts haze in landscapes, giving sharper image with better colour saturation		

*This list of filter factors and the related increase in aperture is based on normal daylight. When the colour temperature changes, in the evening, for instance, these factors will change.

Coloured filters provide the necessary contrast control in black-and-white photography. The tomato appears light on the left-hand side of the picture, because a red filter was used. Compare this with the opposite side of the picture, where it is the lettuce which is lighter, the result of a green filter being used.

ABOVE A red filter holds back green.

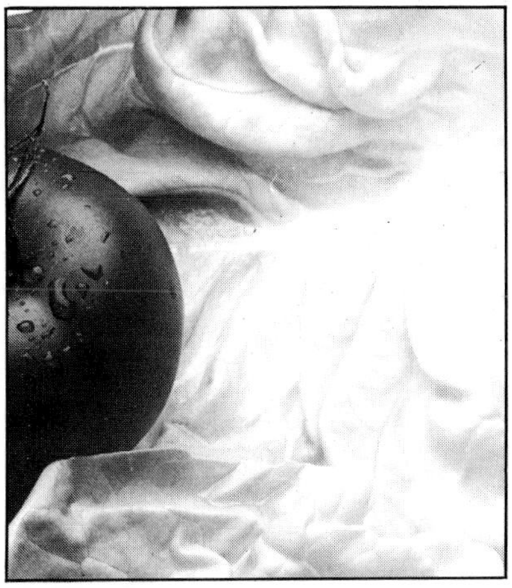

ABOVE A green filter, being the complementary of red, passes green but blocks red.

ILFORD
19A
19
18A
18

BASIC TECHNIQUE

Processing black-and-white film is one of the simplest procedures in photography, and certainly easier and quicker than processing colour materials. There are five stages: developing, stop bath, fixing, washing and drying. By the time the processing is about to begin, the film has been exposed, and carries what is known a a 'latent' image. Those silver halide crystals that have been struck by light have undergone a very small reaction that needs the help of a developing solution before it can be seen.

The developer acts on the exposed crystals, and converts them into metallic silver, which is black and stable. The timing controls the quantity of black silver, and if the film were left in the developer too long, the image would eventually be obliterated. So, once the developer has acted for long enough, it is poured away and replaced with a stop bath. This completely halts any more development, and is a good idea because, even with the tank freshly emptied, drops of developer remain on the emulsion. Following this, the fixing solution dissolves away the remaining unexposed silver halide crystals. Washing removes all traces of fixer and the dissolved halides, and must be thorough, or else the image that the negative carries will not stay permanent.

For equipment and materials, look back to the earlier section of this book. In addition to these basic items, you will need the following chemical solutions: developer; stop bath; fixer; and a recommended optional extra – wetting agent. Of these, there is an important choice only in the developer. Several manufacturers produce solutions that are essentially similar in action, and the most convenient choice is usually the one recommended in the instruction leaflet packed with the film.

Developers are supplied in powder or liquid concentrates, and must be mixed and diluted before use. Normally, there are two alternative methods of use: to mix just enough for the number of films you intend to develop, discarding the used developer each time; or making up a larger quantity and re-using it. If you re-use developer, the time must be increased progressively. For instance, with Kodak's D-76, a typical standard developer, The first two uses can be performed at the recommended time, the next two for 6% longer, and the fifth and sixth for 12% longer. After that, throw the solution away. With this method, which saves money, you must keep a careful note on the storage bottle of how often it has been used.

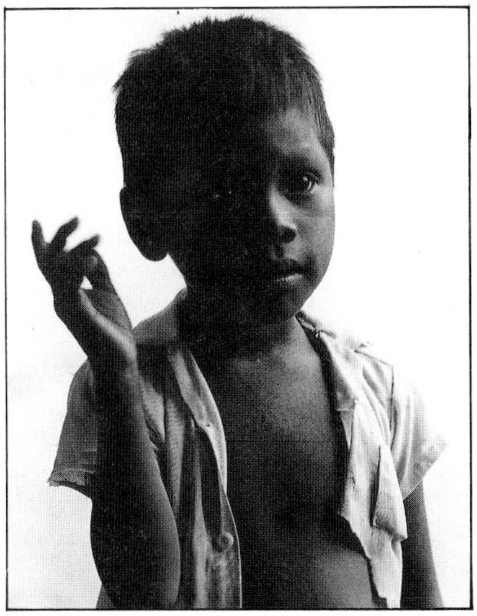

ABOVE The production of a visible black and white image is a simple matter of realising the 'latent' image already present on the exposed frame of film. This is achieved by immersing the film in developer, which acts on exposed silver halide crystals, converting them into metallic silver, which is black and stable.

LEFT Examining negative strips is easiest on a light box; the large format negative is going to cause some difficulties in printing, because of the extreme contrast in the original scene.

BASIC PROCESSING

First of all, read the instructions that come with the developer very carefully. There are two important variables that are linked – the development time and the temperature – and the leaflet will show your choices. The normal temperature for black-and-white films is 20°C (68°F), but there is a range cooler and warmer than this that can be used, provided that you adjust the development time. Typically, for each 2 degrees C (3.6°F) cooler, add 10% to the time, and for each 2 degrees C warmer (3.6°F), develop for 10% less time. The workable temperature range is normally from about 18-24°C (64-75°F).

Plan the times from the point at which the tank has been filled to the point at which it has been drained. So, first practice pouring away a solution so that you know how long it will take.

Once you have filled the tank with developer, it needs to be agitated so that the solution acts evenly on all parts of the film. There are a number of techniques, but the most common is that shown, in which the tank is inverted (be sure that the cap is secure on the central filling hole and that you hold the tank in such a way that the lid cannot fall off). If you do not agitate enough, the emulsion will be developed unevenly, but there will be a different type of unevenness, called surge marks, if there is too much agitation.

In place of the stop bath (a mild solution of acetic acid), you could use plain water, although this does not halt the development as quickly. Both this and the fixer can be re-used several times. If it is important to complete the processing quickly, two other things will help. One is a rapid fixer instead of the normal version; the other is a clearing agent called hypo eliminator, which is used after the fix to reduce washing time from 30 to five minutes.

1. First mix the developer to the required dilution, and bring it to 20° C/68°F (or another recommended temperature) by placing the graduated jug in a deep dish of warm water.
2. Pour the developer into the tank. Start the time.
3. Smartly tap the tank on a hard surface to dislodge any air bubbles.
4. Agitate the tank as recommended.

BELOW Certain basic precautions can, if taken, make the difference between success and disaster. These include using clean graduates, mixing powdered chemicals thoroughly and ensuring correct solution strength. When loading film, check the drum lid is secure to prevent light leaks, and that the film is not buckled mid-frame when being loaded.

Preserving Chemicals

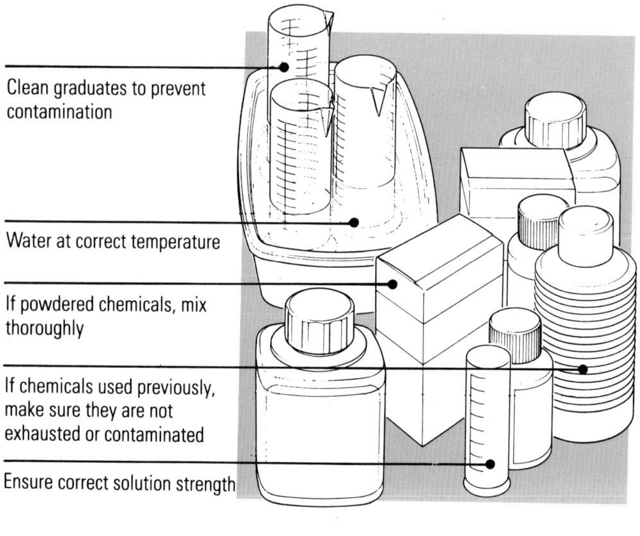
Clean graduates to prevent contamination
Water at correct temperature
If powdered chemicals, mix thoroughly
If chemicals used previously, make sure they are not exhausted or contaminated
Ensure correct solution strength

Loading Film

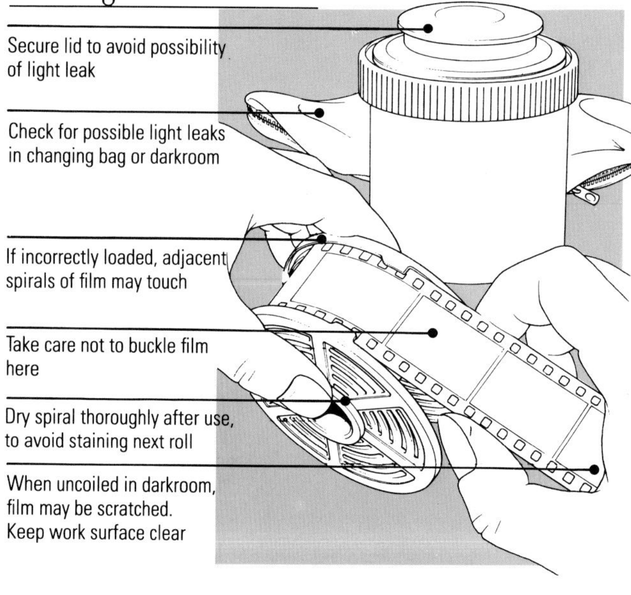
Secure lid to avoid possibility of light leak
Check for possible light leaks in changing bag or darkroom
If incorrectly loaded, adjacent spirals of film may touch
Take care not to buckle film here
Dry spiral thoroughly after use, to avoid staining next roll
When uncoiled in darkroom, film may be scratched. Keep work surface clear

Black-and-White Film Processing Procedure

Before beginning black and white processing, there are a number of important points to remember. Firstly, it is important that all chemicals are fresh. Secondly, ensure that your darkroom is completely light proof; too many films are ruined by light leaks. Lastly, ensure that the film is well agitated in the developer solution.

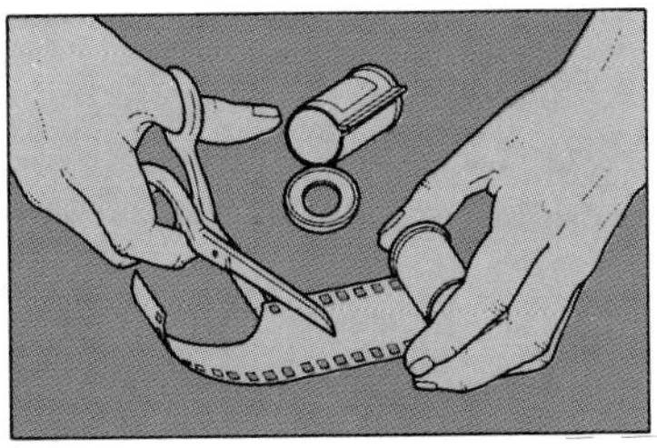

1. In complete darkness, open the cassette by prising off the end with a bottle opener or special cassette opener. Take out the film and cut off the tongue.

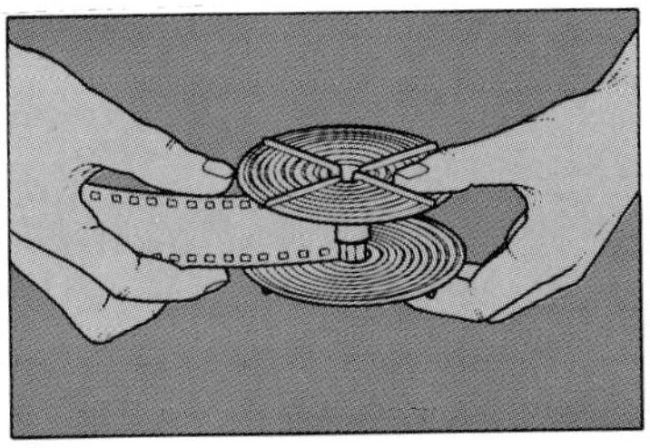

2. Holding the film by its edges, bow it carefully and attach the end to the spike or clip at the core of the stainless steel reel. Rotate the reel so that the film is pulled out along the special grooves and thread the film inwards from rim.

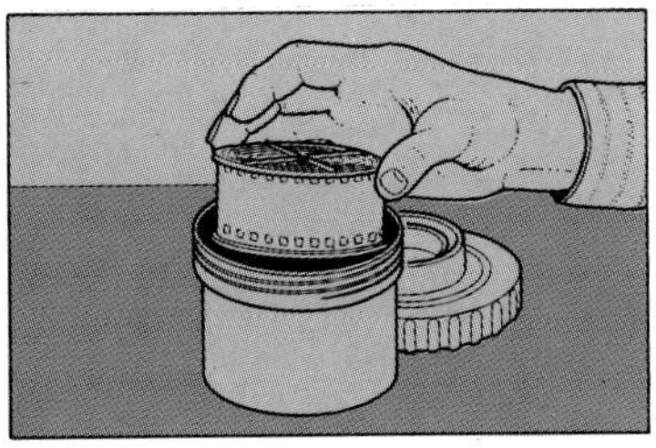

3. Trim off the end of the film that was attached to the cassette spool, lower the loaded reel into the developer tank and replace the lid. The room light can now be switched on.

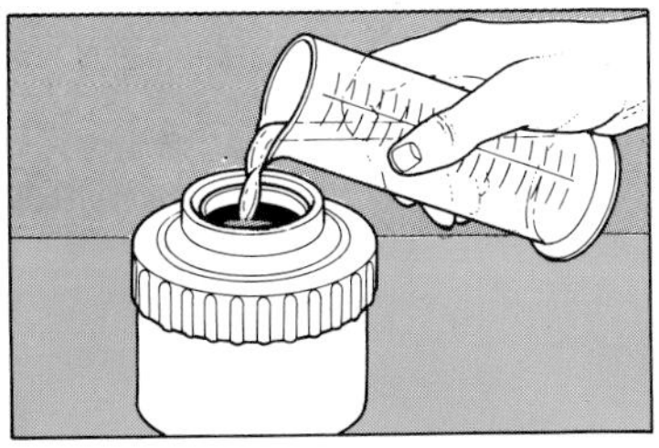

4. Having checked the temperature of the developer solution, pour it quickly into the tank. When full, tap the tank to dislodge air bubbles, and fit the cap that covers the lid's central opening.

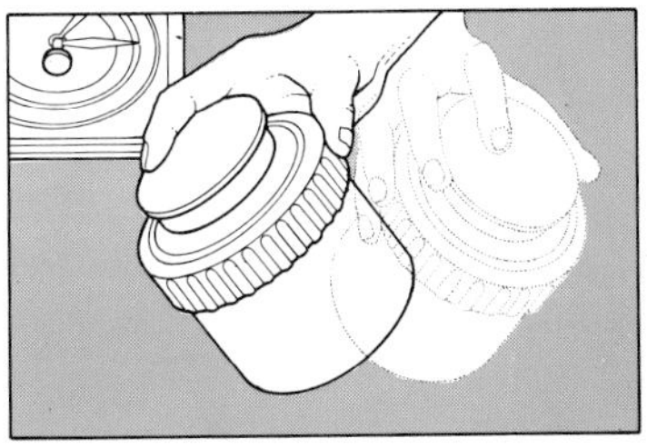

5. Trip the timer switch. During development, agitate the tank by rocking it backwards and forwards to ensure even application of the solution. Agitate for 15 seconds every minute.

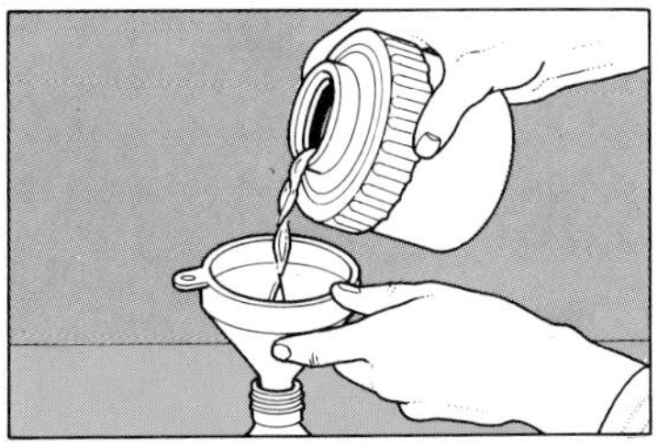

6. At the end of the development time, quickly pour out the developer. Pour in stop bath and agitate continuously for 30 seconds. Pour out and re-fill with fixer for the time recommended by the manufacturer.

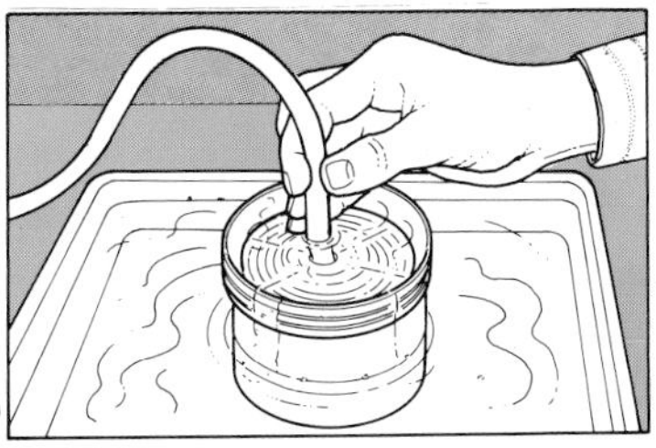

7. When the fixing period is over, empty the tank, take off the lid and insert a hose from the cold water tap into the core of the reel. Wash for at least 30 minutes in gently running water. Strong water pressure may damage the emulsion.

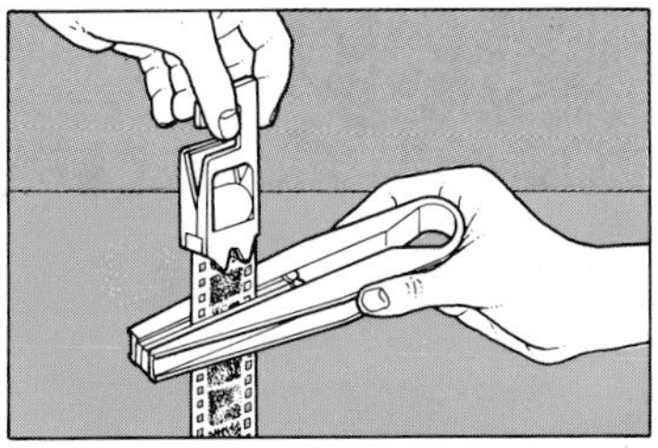

8. Before removing the reel from the tank, add a few drops of wetting agent to avoid drying marks. Attach film to a hanger clip, pull out and gently wipe off the bulk of the moisture. Hang to dry in a space free from dust and air movement.

5. Pour away the developer about 10 seconds before the end of time – or at least, so that the timer finishes just as the tank is emptied.
6. Pour in stop bath or water. Agitate as recommended.
7. Return the stop bath to its container at the end of the set time.
8. Pour in fixer and agitate as recommended.
9. Return the fixer to its bottle for further use.
10. Remove the tank's lid and wash the film by inserting a short length of hose into the core of the reel.
11. When the wash is complete, add a few drops of wetting agent. This checks the risk of drying marks.
12. Attach a film clip to the exposed end of the film, and pull out from its reel.
13. Hang the film on a clothes line, weighting the lower end with a second clip. Run a wetted sponge or squeegee down the strip to remove drops of water.

ALTERING FILM QUALITIES

Deliberate over- and under-exposure not only affect the density of the negative, but the contrast also. This is a valuable technique for controlling the image and is, incidentally, an important part of using the Zone System described earlier. Because there are only tones to think about, altered development is a much simpler and more useful technique in black-and-white than it could ever be in colour.

If you increase the development, the tonal range is expanded, and so the contrast is increased. If, on the other hand, the development is decreased, the

If the aim is to reduce contrast from the average (below), then the tonal range may be compressed by decreasing the development of the print (left).

RIGHT If development of a print is increased, the tonal range is expanded, with the result that contrast is boosted.

Altering Film Development

Under-development lowers contrast and so extends the tonal range (far right). Over-development increases contrast, compressing the tonal range. (right). Therefore, with a high contrast subject, where bright highlights and dense shadows cannot both be recorded on a normally processed negative, under-developing the film (by shortening the time or diluting the chemicals) will help. To compensate, the exposure will have had to have been increased. On the other hand, if the subject is flat, increasing the development (by extending the time, raising the temperature or increasing the concentration of developer) will make the image more lively. In this case, the exposure must have been reduced. For this type of contrast control, adjustments in the order of a half or one f-stop are normally made.

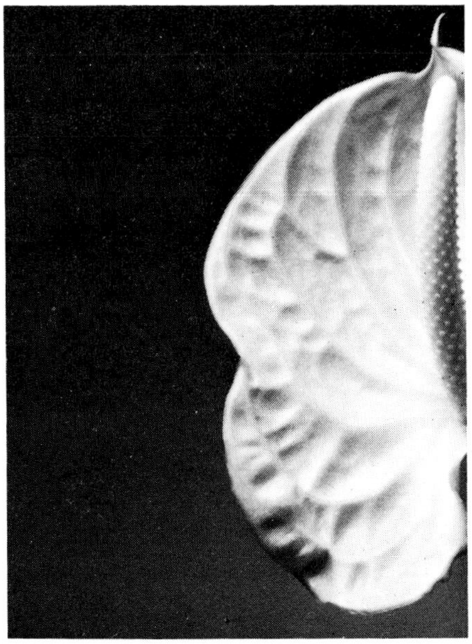

tonal range is compressed and the contrast reduced. This means, for example, that a scene with a limited range of tones, such as on a dull day, can be given more life by push-processing the film. If you are using this technique only to control the contrast, remember to adjust the exposure setting accordingly. Should you plan to reduce contrast by under-developing one stop, for instance, the lens aperture will have to be opened up or the shutter speed slowed down by the equivalent amount. Alternatively, you could alter the film speed rating: for one-stop underdevelopment of Tri-X or HP5, rate them at ISO200 instead of ISO400.

The actual procedure varies according to the film/developer combination, and there is even some choice. There are three things that affect the degree of development: the development time; the temperature; and the strength of the developer solution. In theory, changing any of these will do the job, but the limits are set by the need for an evenly processed image. Under-development in particular is limited by this, and for this reason it may be better to use a special low-contrast developer; development times should be at least more than 5 minutes. Overall, the most commonly used technique is altering the time (this is the only practical choice available to a professional lab, which is processing quantities of film at a time, most of it normal).

Altered Processing

EFFECT	DEVELOPER	DEV. TIME	TEMP	DILUTION
−2	Low activity dev. eg Perceptol	N	N	½ strength
−1	Low activity dev. eg Perceptol	N	N	N
	or Normal dev. eg D-76	less 30%	N	N
N	Normal dev. eg D-76	N	N	N
+1	Normal dev. eg D-76	add 30%	N	N
+2	Normal dev. eg D-76	add 75%	N	N
+3	Normal dev. eg D-76	add 160%	N	N

SPEED vs CONTRAST

Because altered processing changes both the strength and contrast of the image, it is important to be clear about the effect that you want. Push-processing can be used as a technique for photographing in low light or for higher contrast, or for both. The film speed is adjustable, but the increase in contrast is inevitable, as is an increase in grain. In particular, the shadow areas (those which receive least exposure and so are palest in the negative) tend to lose detail, and block up into solid areas of black when the negative is printed. Graininess, as we saw earlier, becomes most obvious in mid-toned areas.

For maximum film speed, select a fast film to begin with, as push-processing a slow or medium film is always less effective than using a film that has been designed for its great sensitivity to light. On the other hand, if you want only to increase the contrast, it is more effective if you choose a slow film – this is already slightly more contrasty than faster emulsions.

Pull-processing is less commonly used, simply because of the circumstances in which most photographs are taken. There is insufficient light for photography more often than there is too much, and the requirement for high contrast in a scene is more usual than lowering it.

Although all of the above assumes that you have planned to change the development from the start, these are also useful emergency procedures in cases where you have made an exposure mistake. The most common is forgetting to change the meter setting or film speed dial when changing film types. If this happens, simply continue shooting at the 'wrong' setting (provided that it is within a correctable range, between about 2 stops under and 3 stops over), and make the adjustments to the development.

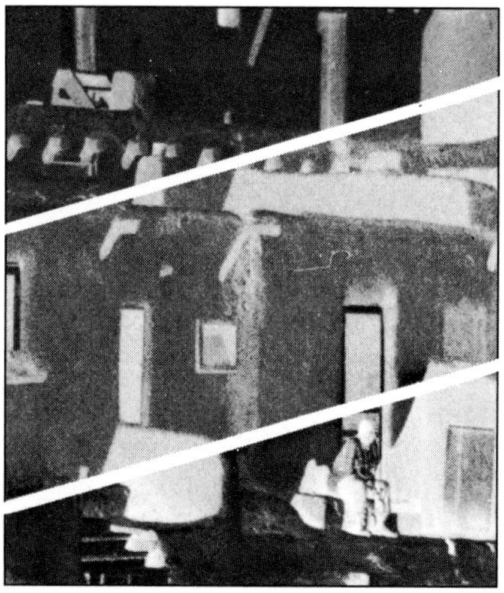

Under-development gives low contrast (above), over-development gives high (above right). The second shot had been under-exposed to allow for over-development.

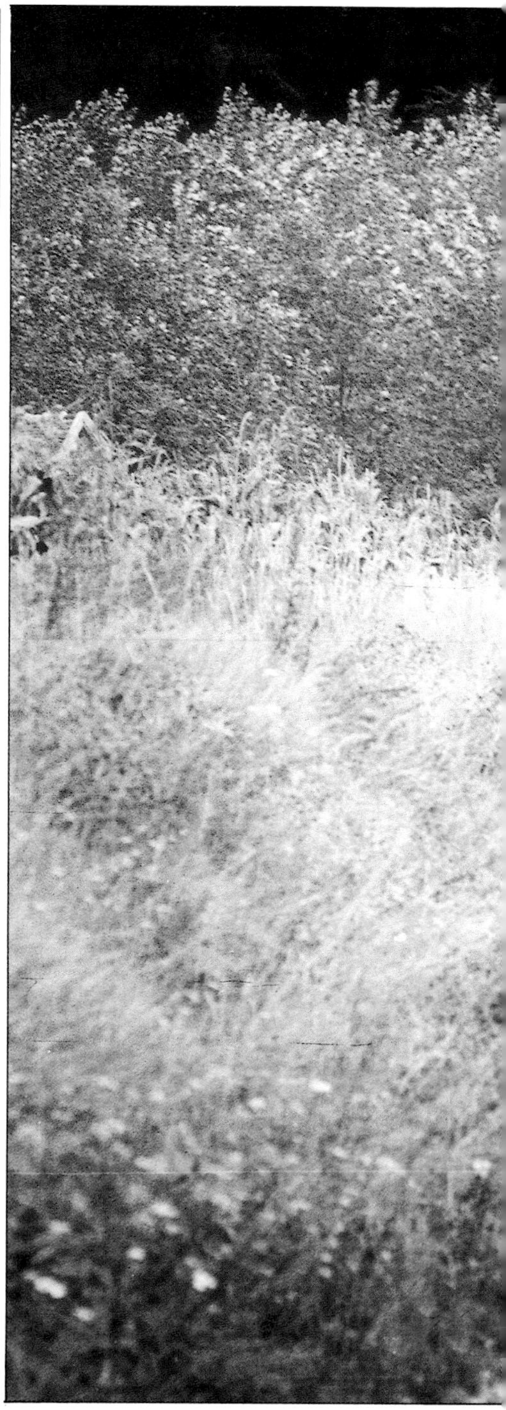

ABOVE One by-product of the increase in contrast that results from push-processing is a loss of detail in shadow areas, which tend to block into solid black. Graininess, meanwhile, becomes most obvious in mid-toned areas.

FAULTS & EMERGENCIES

When things go wrong, the time to discover them is usually at the end of the processing. The first check that you should make when the film is dry and ready to handle is for gross errors. The transparent edges of black-and-white negative film – called the rebates – make it a little easier to spot mistakes than on colour transparency film, as does the contrast range, which is generally lower. Unwanted exposure, such as light leaks and flaring, appear as dark areas on the negative, while parts that have been blocked from the light appear clear. Because commercial processing is now geared to colour film, black-and-white development by other people, when you can find it, is not infrequently at a lower standard; this is one of the strongest arguments for doing your own processing.

Faults can occur in three areas of the photography, and it is important to identify which applies to a particular error. The three areas are: the condition of the film; the exposure; and the processing. The first of these is the least

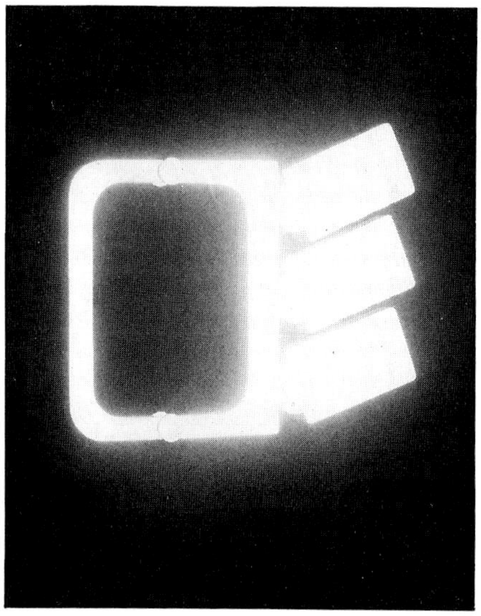

ABOVE A bad case of over-exposure during printing such as this can be easily rectified . . . by throwing it away and making another print!

LEFT If a print is found to suffer from blurring, such as here, there are two potential causes. The first is that the camera may have moved during the original exposure, and unfortunately there is no easy cure here – unless you're willing to enter into a lengthy retouching exercise! The other possible cause is that the enlarger may have been jolted. Fortunately, the cure here is quite simple – make another print.

LEFT When corresponding to the positioning of the sprockets on the film strip, light leaks (top of the print) can be turned to your advantage. This can be done by 'burning in'; darkening an area of the print during the enlarging process by placing a block between light source and paper.

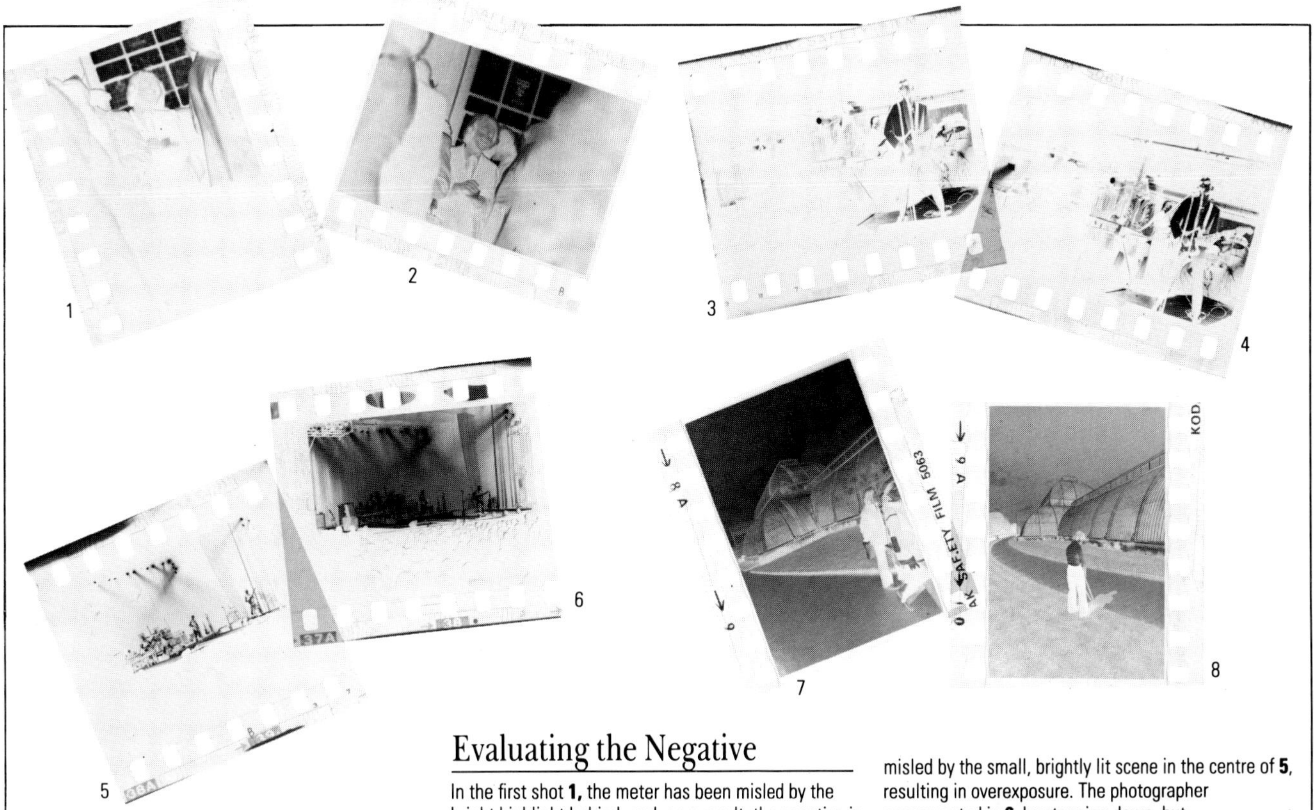

Evaluating the Negative

In the first shot **1**, the meter has been misled by the bright highlight behind, and, as a result, the negative is underexposed. There is more detail in **2**, and it would be much easier to print, **3** and **4** have a 2-stop exposure difference between them. Note how the piano player, who is virtually invisible in **3**, appears when the exposure has been opened up. The metering has been misled by the small, brightly lit scene in the centre of **5**, resulting in overexposure. The photographer compensated in **6**, by stopping down, but underdevelopment has aggravated the problem, causing burned out highlights. Negative **7** has a heavy sky (it was blue) and would print flat white. The sky area in **8** would print much darker because the photographer had fitted a red filter to the lens.

An ill-defined dark area is characteristic of accidental exposure to light. Here, this includes the rebate, suggesting that the leak occurred outside the camera (top). Two adjacent pieces of the film stuck together in the developing tank, preventing full exposure to the processing solutions (above).

likely, but includes manufacturing defects and bad storage. While photographers, and even some camera manufacturers, are ready to identify the film makers as the culprits in many situations, the truth is that defects are very rare. More often than not, the cause of the fault lies in the camera, the way it is used, and in the darkroom.

The examples that follow are some of the most typical, and are intended to help you identify ones that you may come across. There are not many generalizations that are useful, but one is this: if the blemish, or whatever form the fault takes, extends beyond the rectangle of the picture frame, it has almost certainly not occurred during the exposure. The rebates themselves can offer quite a lot of information, particularly about the processing. These rebates carry printed frame numbers and the film's name, and as this has been pre-exposed by the manufacturer, it is consistent. In other words, if this lettering appears either weak or dense, it indicates a processing, rather than an exposure, error.

Processing errors usually happen because the photographer was not paying full attention, or through inexperience. Always make an effort to find out exactly what happened – the only positive value of a mistake is that you can in future avoid doing the same thing.

Some faults can be cured or concealed, by retouching, special treatment, or in the printing. Only throw away a damaged negative if you are absolutely sure that you can make nothing of it.

Fogging in camera: opaque areas may be visible at the edges of the film, though the middle should be clear.

Scratching: parallel scratches indicate grit either on the film cassette mouth or in the squeegee used to dry the film.

Fogging: opaque areas that should be clean and clear, almost certainly due to light reaching the film while loading into the tank. All-over density throughout the film could also be fogging of a different sort. This could be the remains of silver halide still in the emulsion which has not been "cleared" by fixing. A re-fix can cure the problem. **Undeveloped strip:** down one side of film, caused by insufficient developer in the tank. All the film must be immersed under the developer. If one film is developed in a two-spiral tank, it is possible for the single spiral to move upward during agitation. Use the securing device supplied with the tank.

EMERGENCY TECHNIQUES

If the film has been over- or under-exposed, choice of paper grade and a different exposure in the enlarger will help to an extent, but the negative can also be intensified or reduced in special chemicals. If the negative has been scratched, it may still be possible to make a good print by temporarily coating the emulsion with a thin layer of glycerin. This fills in the scratches and has a refractive index similar to that of the gelatin in the emulsion. If this does not work you will have to retouch the print; negative retouching is only practical on a large sheet of film.

VIEWING THE NEGATIVE

In order to be able to make a proper assessment of a negative, you must be in a position to study it closely and with efficient back-lighting. The ideal equipment is a light box and a loupe; proprietary light boxes use fluorescent strip-lights backed with white reflecting metal or plastic, covered with a sheet of translucent plastic. They are relatively expensive, but it is fairly straightforward

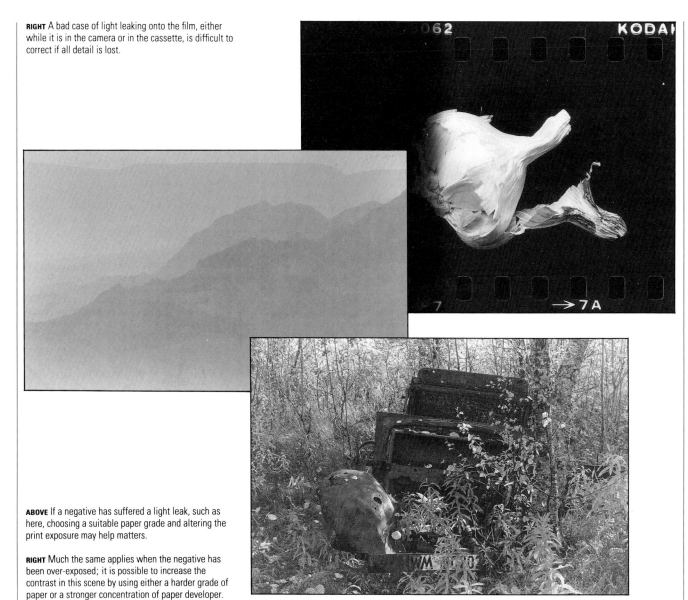

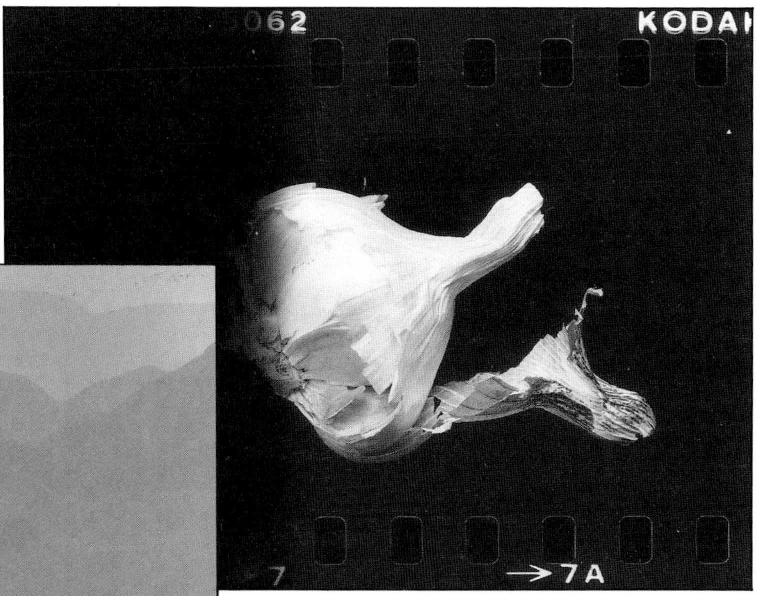

RIGHT A bad case of light leaking onto the film, either while it is in the camera or in the cassette, is difficult to correct if all detail is lost.

ABOVE If a negative has suffered a light leak, such as here, choosing a suitable paper grade and altering the print exposure may help matters.

RIGHT Much the same applies when the negative has been over-exposed; it is possible to increase the contrast in this scene by using either a harder grade of paper or a stronger concentration of paper developer.

to build your own. The important criterion is that the illumination is even, yet bright.

Not even a home-made light box is entirely necessary. A plain white sheet of paper illuminated by an ordinary desk lamp aimed downwards is effective and simple; if you then support a plain sheet of glass over this (on two piles of books, for instance), the negative strip can be laid flat for close examination with a loupe.

■ ASSESSING THE NEGATIVE

Faults apart, an assessment of the density and contrast of the negative will help in planning the print, which we deal with on the following pages. Experience in looking at many different negatives, and then printing them, will show what standard density and normal contrast are. For now, one simple guide to density is to press the negative flat down on a sheet of printed white paper, such as the page of a book. If the exposure and development have been normal, the lettering should just be visible through the darkest areas in the negative.

PLANNING THE PRINT

In black-and-white photography, the print is the end-product, and if you know exactly what choices and controls are available to you in the darkroom, you will be able to shoot more effectively. Experienced black-and-white photographers visualise the final print when they are setting up a shot.

First, printing allows selective enlargement. You do not have to stay with the full negative frame, or with your original composition. Instead, you can crop the image to exclude parts that are distracting or irrelevant, and to concentrate on the main components. You can keep the same general proportions of the picture, or experiment by setting the enlarger easel to an unusual shape: for example, a long horizontal frame for a low, panoramic landscape. While it can become sloppy technique to rely always on darkroom decisions to make successful images, many people find that they can make more effective compositions when they have the time to consider an already-shot photograph.

Having chosen how to crop the negative, and the size of enlargement, there is then considerable choice in overall density, overall contrast, and in the relative tones between different areas of the image. These are determined by the exposure, the choice of paper, and the developing technique (strength and temperature of the developer, and how long it is allowed to act on the print).

So much can be done at this stage of making a photograph that there is a temptation to be less careful when shooting – to rely on the darkroom stage to make the photograph successful. This certainly works, but is rather a waste of darkroom skills, which can be used to better effect for making delicate improvements to a good negative.

Choosing and Using

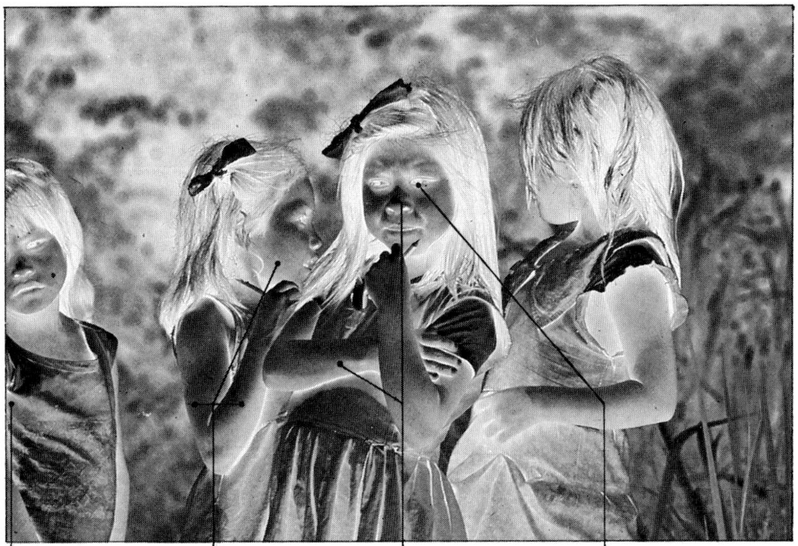

In the print crop out this girl as only half her face appears.

Key tones are the faces and arms of the girls.

Be careful in printing not to block highlights on these areas.

The shadow detail in the eyes needs to be retained.

BELOW When compared with the low-contrast example (bottom), changing to glossy paper brings a noticeable increase in contrast.

ABOVE Printing on a low-contrast, matt-surfaced paper is a sure-fire method of ensuring a low-contrast print.

LEFT Note how, when compared with the print below, the shadow over the doorway in this scene has lost all detail. This has been achieved by dodging – preventing light from reaching the print.

BELOW If you are looking for stark, high contrasts, then choose a high-contrast, glossy white printing paper.

■ OVERALL DENSITY

This is controlled principally by altering the exposure in the enlarger and, just as there is often no single 'correct' exposure when shooting, most negatives can be printed lighter or darker according to taste. Although either the aperture or the time can be adjusted, most darkroom workers find it easier to leave the aperture at a fixed setting and give several seconds more or less. Further density control is possible in the development but, as with film, changes here also affect contrast.

■ OVERALL CONTRAST

The usual method of setting this is by selecting an appropriate paper grade, but the paper texture and tint also contribute. A glossy surface (which gives the deepest black) and white paper stock (which gives the brightest highlights) help to produce the highest contrast.

■ LOCAL CONTRAST

This can be adjusted by allowing more light to some parts of the print and less to others.

CHOOSING THE PAPER

Interestingly, printing papers are available in a wider range of characteristics than black-and-white film. Apart from size, printing papers come in different paper thicknesses, textures, tints, tones, types of coating and, probably most important of all, contrast grades. Speed, however, is not offered as a variable, but the way in which it is used renders such a choice unimportant. There is no difficulty in altering the exposure by almost any degree, unlike many camera situations. In order to allow workable exposure times of at least a few seconds, paper sensitivity to light is less than that of film.

CONTRAST GRADE

To compensate for low or high contrast in the negative, paper is available in several grades of contrast. The normal grade is 2, low-contrast is 1 (for contrasty negatives), and high-contrast grades are 3 and 4 (for flat negatives). This is the basic range, but some paper manufacturers produce a 0 grade – extremely low contrast – and a 5 grade, which is very high, or 'hard'.

An alternative is variable-contrast paper – a single type that will give a range depending on whether a bluish or yellowish filter is used in the enlarger. The advantage of this is that you need only buy one stock of paper.

WEIGHT

This is a measure of paper thickness. The most commonly available are single weight and double weight, the latter being better for significant enlargement because it has less tendency to crease or buckle.

TEXTURE

This refers to both the smoothness of the surface and to textural patterns introduced for special effect. The smoother the surface, the less scattering of light there is, and the deeper the blacks. So, for a good range of contrast and rich shadow tones, glossy paper is for many photographers the ideal. Except for resin-coated (RC) paper, this can be 'ferrotyped' by drying it in contact with a smooth metal plate to give an even glossier effect, but an unglazed finish is more usual. Common alternatives to glossy are matte, lustre and pearl.

In addition, special papers are made to imitate the surface of an oil canvas, silk, and so on.

TINT

White paper is normal, giving the most brilliance in highlights, but slightly tinted stock, such as cream, is also available.

TONE

The mixture of chemicals in the emulsion determines the exact tone of the dark parts of the image, which can tend towards blue-black, brown-black, warm-black, or may just be neutral.

COATING

An alternative to standard, paper-base paper, and one that is becoming increasingly popular, is resin-coating. These papers have a water-resistant base that confines the processing chemicals to the emulsion and speeds up the fixing, washing and drying.

RIGHT While it is almost impossible to illustrate different paper finishes in print, the examples shown here may give some idea how great a difference the paper and finish can make to the final result, when development is the same for each print. One of the most obvious effects is the scattering of light on a textured surface (such as the linen bases shown here) which results in shallower blacks. For rich shadow tones, glossy papers are therefore preferred.

TOP, FROM RIGHT TO LEFT resin-coated glossy; Kentmere textured matt; Ilford Galerie; (middle) fibre-based glossy, unglazed; tinted linen base; white linen; (bottom) Chlorobromide fibre-based, matt; fibre-based glossy, unglazed; Chlorobromide fibre-based glossy, unglazed.

1

2

3

4

5

6

7

8

9

ABOVE Contact sheets are both easy to produce and provide a quick means for assessing your negatives. To make the most of the sheets, however, it is wise to invest in a magnifier of some description.

THE CONTACT SHEET

A contact sheet, also known as a proof sheet, is a print of several negatives made without enlargement and used as a visual reference. This is both a record of your black-and-white pictures and an aid to selecting a negative for making an enlargement. Normally, all the negatives from one roll of film are printed on a single contact sheet, and this is usually the first thing that is done after the film has been processed.

The equipment and materials are, more or less, those for normal printing. One extra item is a contact printing frame, or at least a sheet of glass for pressing down the negative strips onto the printing paper. An enlarger is not necessary for this stage but, as the point of making a contact sheet is to prepare for printing, you might as well use the enlarger as a light source.

First prepare the chemicals: developer, stop bath and fixer. If you intend to continue with a printing session, make sufficient quantities for a number of prints.

MAKING A CONTACT PRINT

1. Using a graduate, mix each solution in turn, washing the graduate thoroughly between mixings. The developer at least should be at 20°C; the stop bath and fixer can be between 18 and 24°C.
2. Fill three trays with the solutions to a depth of about ½in. Arrange them in order and, if you need the remainder, label them.
3. Turn the safelight on and the room light off. Wash and dry your hands.
4. Adjust the enlarger so that, with no negative in the carrier and de-focused, it illuminates an area large enough to cover the contact printing frame.

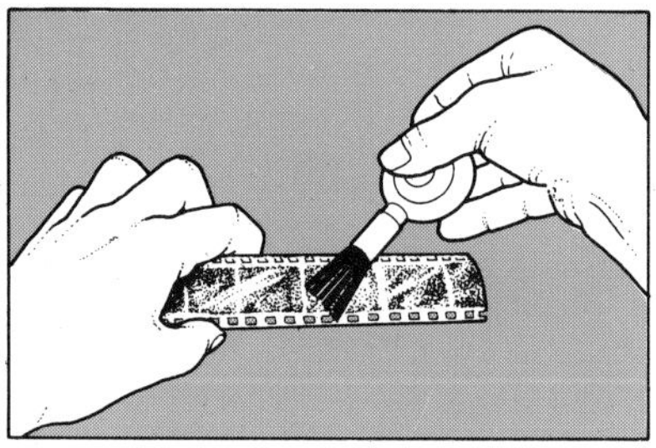

Clean with an airbrush the strip of negatives that you wish to make a contact sheet from.

Ensure that the contact printing frame is free from dust and grit that may show on the contact sheet.

Arrange the clean strips of negatives in the printing frame, emulsion side down.

Adjust the enlarger so that, with no negative in the carrier and de-focused, it illuminates an area large enough to cover the printing frame.

Ensure that your printing paper is placed emulsion side up on the base of the contact printing frame.

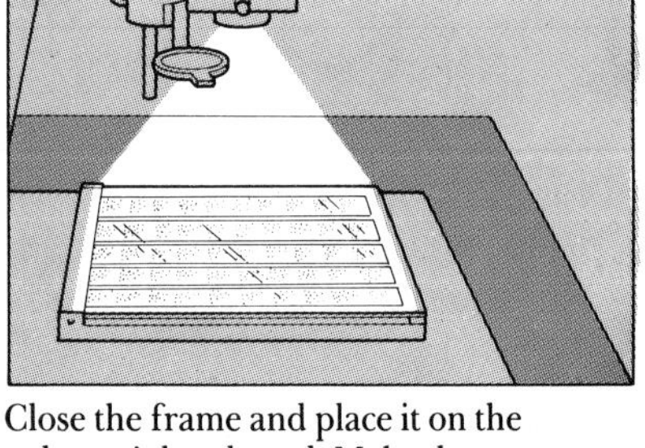

Close the frame and place it on the enlarger's baseboard. Make the exposure, and remember that here it may be necessary to experiment.

5. Remove one sheet of paper from its box and place it, emulsion side up, on the base of the contact printing frame. Arrange the negative strips on top, emulsion side down.
6. Close the frame, and place it on the enlarger's baseboard. Make the exposure (you will need to experiment with this the first time).
7. Remove the paper, slide it into the developer, and rock the tray gently for one minute.
8. Using tongs, take the paper out of the developer, drain it for a few seconds and slide it into the stop bath. Rock the tray for several seconds.
9. Remove and drain, then slide into the fixer. Agitate repeatedly for about two minutes. You can turn the room light on after 30sec.
10. Remove and wash in running water for about four minutes, with the water at the same temperature as the previous solutions.
11. Dry on a flat surface, having wiped off excess moisture with a squeegee.

TOP AND ABOVE The very fact that a contact sheet image is so small means that any mistakes during the printing or processing will make the picture virtually unviewable. Always ensure that your chemicals are fresh, and that the sheet is thoroughly washed.

BELOW Trying to find the best shot from a sequence in negative form can be – to say the least – tricky, and this is where the contact sheet comes into its own. Once the choice has been made, the negative can be singled out on the sheet by marking it with a soft, erasable pencil such as a chinagraph.

THE TEST PRINT

With the negative and contact sheet at hand, you are ready to select one frame for printing. Once you have chosen the negative, the cropping and the size of the enlargement, the next stage is to find the best overall exposure.

The processing stages are the same as for the contact sheet, except that some photographers like to vary the development time according to how the image comes up. To begin with, however, it is best to stick to a standard procedure: the fewer variables, the easier it is to make adjustments. In any case, prepare all the chemicals as shown on the previous pages.

MAKING A TEST PRINT

1. Prepare the developer, stop bath and fixer to the point of having an ordered row of trays, all at the right temperature.
2. Take the negative strip, hold it by its edges, and place it, emulsion side down, in the enlarger's negative carrier.
3. Remove dust from the negative with a burst of compressed air or a soft anti-static brush. Hold it an angle under the enlarger's light for a close check.

ABOVE Choose from the negative the most important tones and try and cover these with each exposure.

BELOW A standard series of exposure times, from five to twenty seconds, gives a good indication of what the final exposure should be. From the examination of the negative, the central part of the picture with its range of skin tones is the most important, and the test bands were arranged so that the most likely exposure falls in this area. Twenty-second and fifteen-second exposures are too dark, with obvious loss of detail in shadow areas, while five seconds leaves the highlights white and featureless. The ten second exposure is almost right, but perhaps a little too dark.

20sec/f11 15sec/f11 10sec/f11 5sec/f11

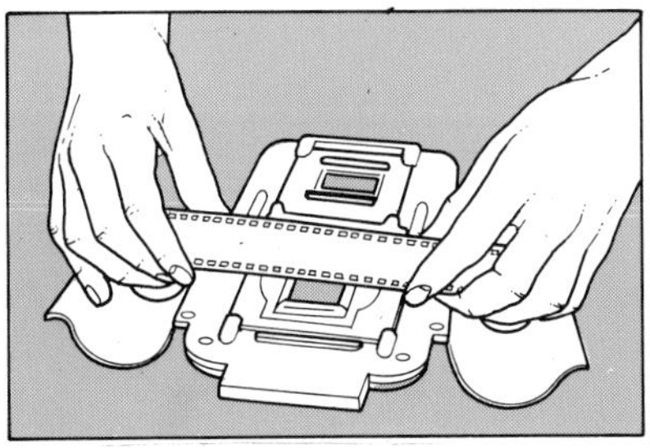

Place the negative in the enlarger's negative carrier (emulsion side down), cleaning off any dust with a blower, anti-static brush or anti-static gun.

Insert the carrier in the enlarger head. With the room lights out, the enlarger head on and the lens aperture wide open, adjust the enlarger head until the image is focused and the size you have chosen.

Adjust the focus until the image is critically sharp. This can be judged either by eye alone or with the use of a magnifier.

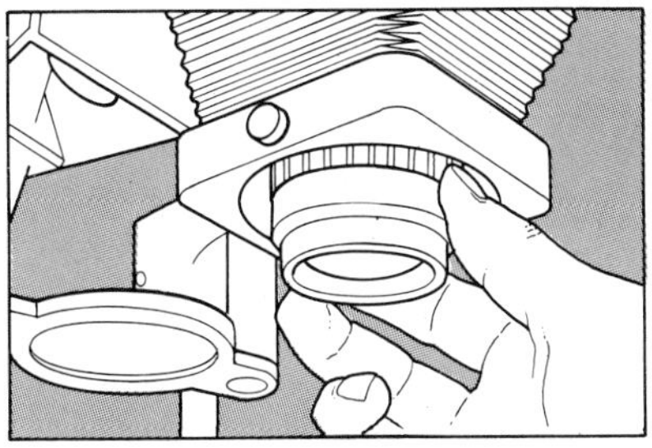

Close down the lens aperture about two stops (normally this would be f11). With a negative of normal density, this will let you use reasonably short exposure times, and the lens performance will be at its peak. Greater depth of field will also compensate for any focusing errors.

Under safelight illumination, and with the enlarger lamp off, insert a sheet of normal (Grade 2) paper, emulsion side up, into the printing frame and set the timer to five seconds.

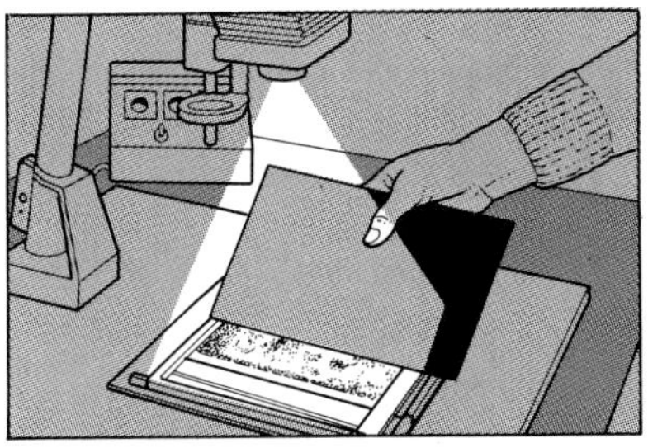

Hold a piece of black card over the sheet of paper, leaving just a quarter of its width exposed, and give a five-second exposure. Move the card along for a second exposure of five seconds. Make third and fourth exposures in the same way.

4. Place a sheet of plain white paper, such as the back of a discarded print, in the easel, and adjust the easel's masks to approximately the proportions that you want. This paper will make composition faster and focusing easier.
5. Turn the safelight on and the room light off. With the lens at full aperture, adjust the enlarger head so that the image fills the frame and is sharply focused.
6. Make final adjustments to the easel masks, as necessary.
7. Reduce the lens aperture by about two stops from fully open. On most lenses this gives the best optical performance.
8. Take a fresh sheet of printing paper and insert it in the easel, emulsion side up, replacing the plain white sheet.
9. Cover all of the exposed paper except for a narrow strip (about 20% of the area) with a piece of thick, opaque card. Make a 5sec exposure.
10. Move the card to uncover a little more of the paper, and give another 5sec exposure. Continue this until all the paper has been exposed (for the last exposure the sheet should be completely uncovered).
11. Process the paper as described earlier, for one minute in the developer, several seconds in the stop bath, and in the fixer for two minutes.
12. Wash and dry.

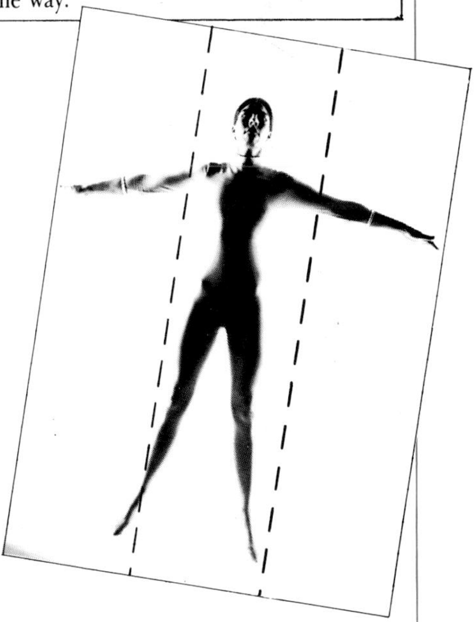

ABOVE The area within the dotted lines marks the most important range of contrasts in this image, from the printer's point of view.

THE FINAL PRINT

With the test print complete, you can now evaluate it and choose the settings for the final print. Study the different exposures – the palest received 5sec, the next 10sec, and so on. Decide which looks best, and set the enlarger timer to this. Also check the test print for dust marks, and if necessary clean the negative again (but do not simply blow air into the enlarger head; that will throw up hidden dust).

At this point you may also decide that some changes are needed to the overall contrast and to local density. Contrast changes are made by choosing a different grade (or a different filter if you are using variable-contrast paper), but there may be a difference in speed between them. If you change from grade 2 to grade 3, for example, the print may need less exposure. The difference will not be great, so it may be sufficient to take a small cut piece of paper and make a single exposure as a test.

If some areas of the print seem to need more or less exposure, you will need to use some of the print controls described earlier. Even so, until you have the experience to be able to predict the exact amount of shading and burning-in, it will probably be easier to make one straight, unmanipulated first print. Then you can examine this to calculate variations in exposure for a later print.

MAKING THE FINAL PRINT

1. Prepare the chemicals as before (although normally, this stage of final printing follows the test print).
2. With the safelight on and the room light off, check the composition and focus once more – particularly if you have removed the negative carrier to remove any more dust.
3. Remove a sheet of paper from its box and insert it in the easel.
4. Make the exposure to the chosen time.
5. Process the paper as before.

The Final Print – Procedure

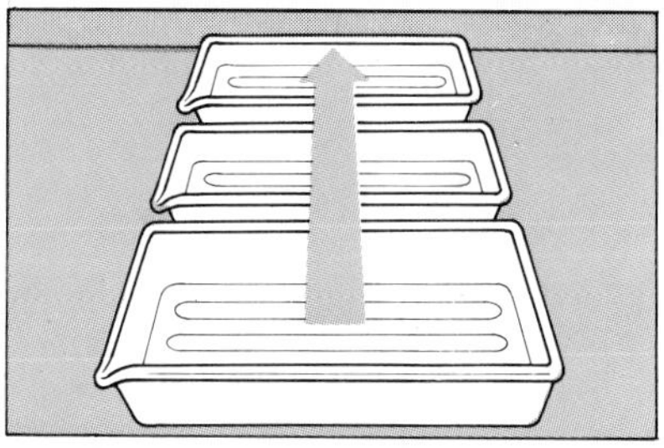

1. Check that the three chemicals – developer, stop bath and fixer – are in the right order, and that the developer is at 20°C (68°F). Make the exposure.

5. Lift the paper out of the developer tray with the tongs and allow excess solution to drip off. Transfer the paper to the stop bath, take care not to dip the develop tongs into the stop bath. Rock the tray as during development.

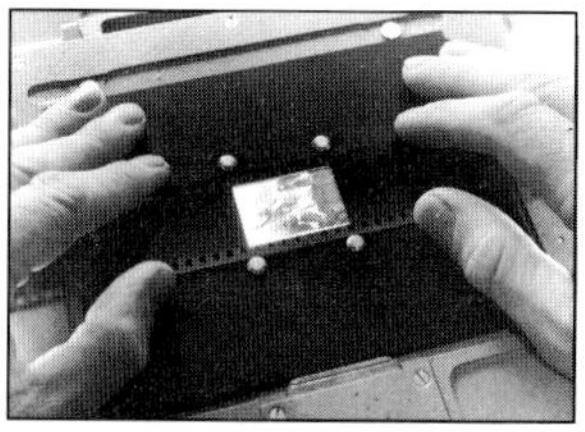

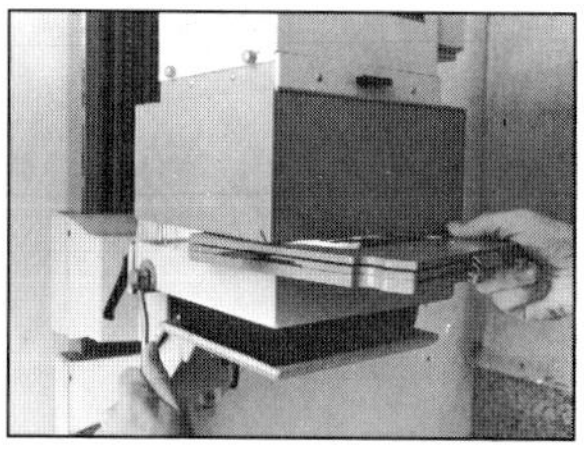

Negative carriers
Glassless negative carriers (**TOP**) are quite adequate for 35mm film but larger formats need glass (**ABOVE**) to hold them flat.

LEFT The final print.

2. Slide the paper, emulsion side down, into the developer tray. Press it down with the developer tongs so that it is fully immersed.

3. Turn the paper over so that the emulsion side is facing up and you can see the developing image.

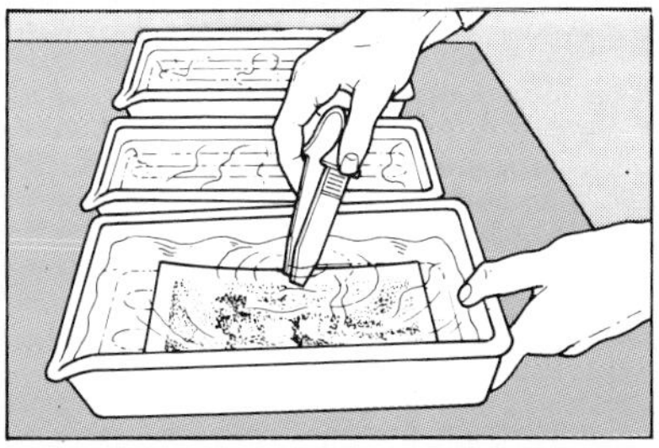

4. Agitate the solution by rocking the tray gently. This ensures that the paper receives even development. Develop for 90 seconds.

6. After 10 secs, lift the print out of the stop bath and drain. Transfer to the fixer, rocking the tray at intervals. After one or two minutes, you can switch on the room lights and examine the print. Leave it in the fixer for at least 10 mins, but no more than 20 mins.

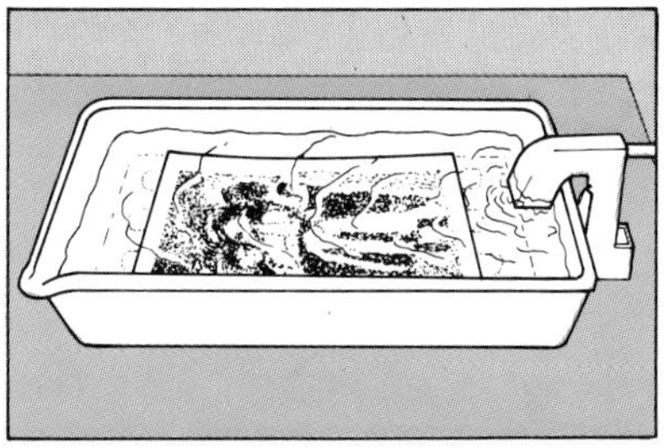

7. Wash the print in running water to remove all traces of the chemicals; washing time varies according to paper manufacturer's recommendations. If the paper is resin-coated, it needs washing for only 4 mins; paper-based papers need about 15 mins.

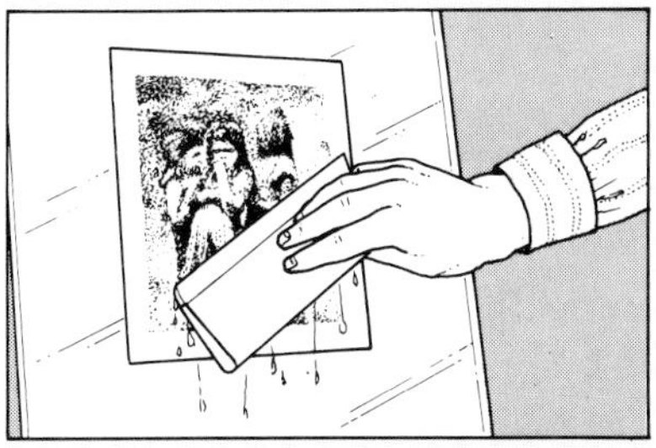

8. Put the print against a smooth flat surface, and wipe off water drops.

Drying the Print

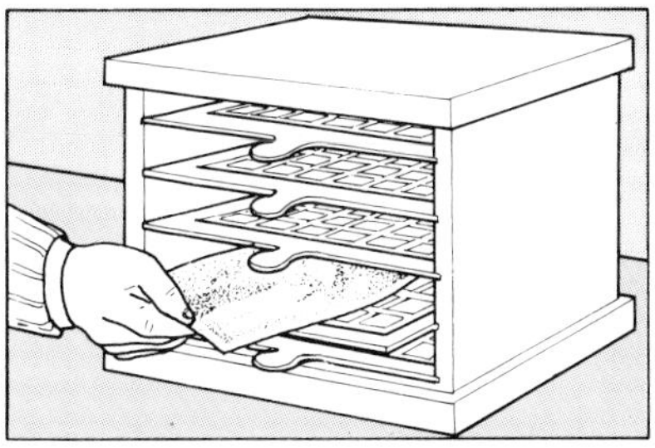

Resin-coated prints. Dry them flat without using a dryer. Air-drying print racks are ideal, as water cannot get trapped underneath the prints.

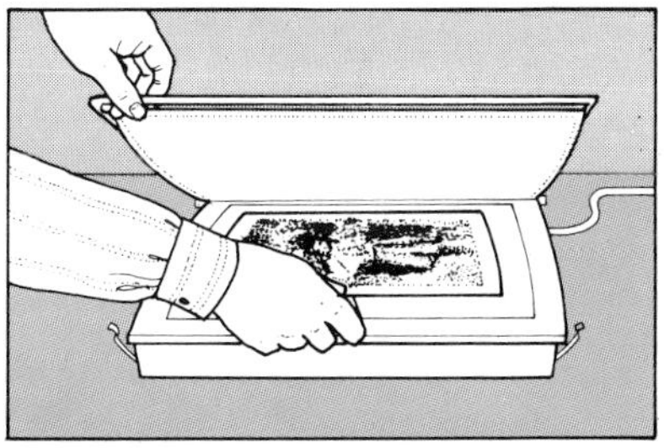

Paper-based prints. These should be dried in a heated dryer (a flatbed machine is normal). Glossy prints can be glazed by being placed face down on the dryer's metal plate. The majority of professional photographers use glossy paper unglazed (ie dried face up).

The usual answer to high contrast, where the range of tones in the negative is beyond that of the print, is to change to a lower contrast grade of paper. This, however, affects the entire image, whereas often it is only local areas that need help. For instance, on an overcast day, in a landscape composed so that there is just a small area of sky, the brightness range below the horizon is likely to be fairly limited. So, for this principal part of the image, a contrast grade of 3, or even 4, would do well, yet the sky would come out a blank white in a straightforward print. Changing to a softer grade of paper would bring the sky within the range of the print's tonal range, but at the serious cost of dullness elsewhere.

Another typical situation which causes uneven brightness across an image is an on-camera flash picture. Because of the position of the flash unit, nearer objects will be brighter than those in the background. If you have not already composed the photograph to take care of this, you will be left with a negative which, if printed normally, has too great a range of tones.

The solution to these and similar problems is to give selected areas of the print more or less exposure than normal, by moving your hands or a shaped piece of card in the path of light from the enlarger lens. Holding back the light from an area is called dodging or shading; giving extra exposure is called burning-in or printing-in.

You can either make or buy printing tools. Dodging tools include large sheets of black card to cover big areas that run over an edge of the frame (such as the sky) and small discs, ovals and other shapes each attached to a length of wire for small areas inside the print (such as faces). The wires are necessary to avoid shading more than a limited area, and in use a dodging tool must be moved constantly, otherwise the shadow of the wire rod will print distinctly.

Tools for burning-in are basically large sheets of black card, each cut with a hole of a particular shape. Again in use they must be moved around all the time to keep the edge projected by the hole soft and indistinct on the print. For this same reason, it is easier to blend the effect of burning-in, or dodging, if the printing tool is held at a distance from the print – the further away it is, the more out of focus the edges will be. Thus, if you are making your own tools, it is often better to keep them fairly small, as raising the tool away from the print will cause it to cover a larger area on the print.

With burning-in, always use a sheet of black card large enough to cover a bigger area than the print; it is surprisingly easy when using this technique to be so absorbed in controlling the patch of light in the middle that you do not notice stray light at the edges of the print.

Rather than prepare several large sheets of black card for burning-in, an alternative is to make one with a fairly large central hole, and to stick over this

Shading-in Technique

1. Your hand may be used to shade the print, although keep it moving to prevent sharp contrasts between affected and unaffected areas.

2. Shading tools are commercially available, these being designed to shade specific areas.

3. Cupped hands may be used to control the size of the area during printing in.

BELOW The blocking out technique is very popular in industrial product photography, and involves holding back light from an area of the print to give a 'cut-out' effect.

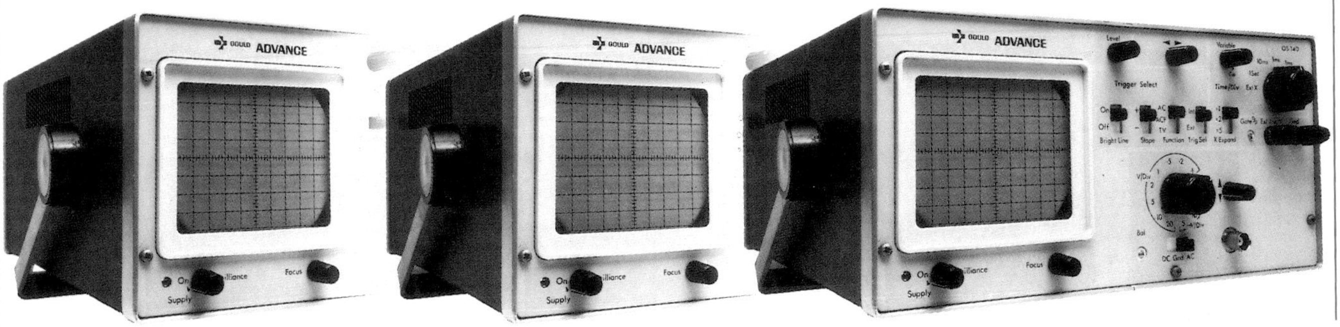

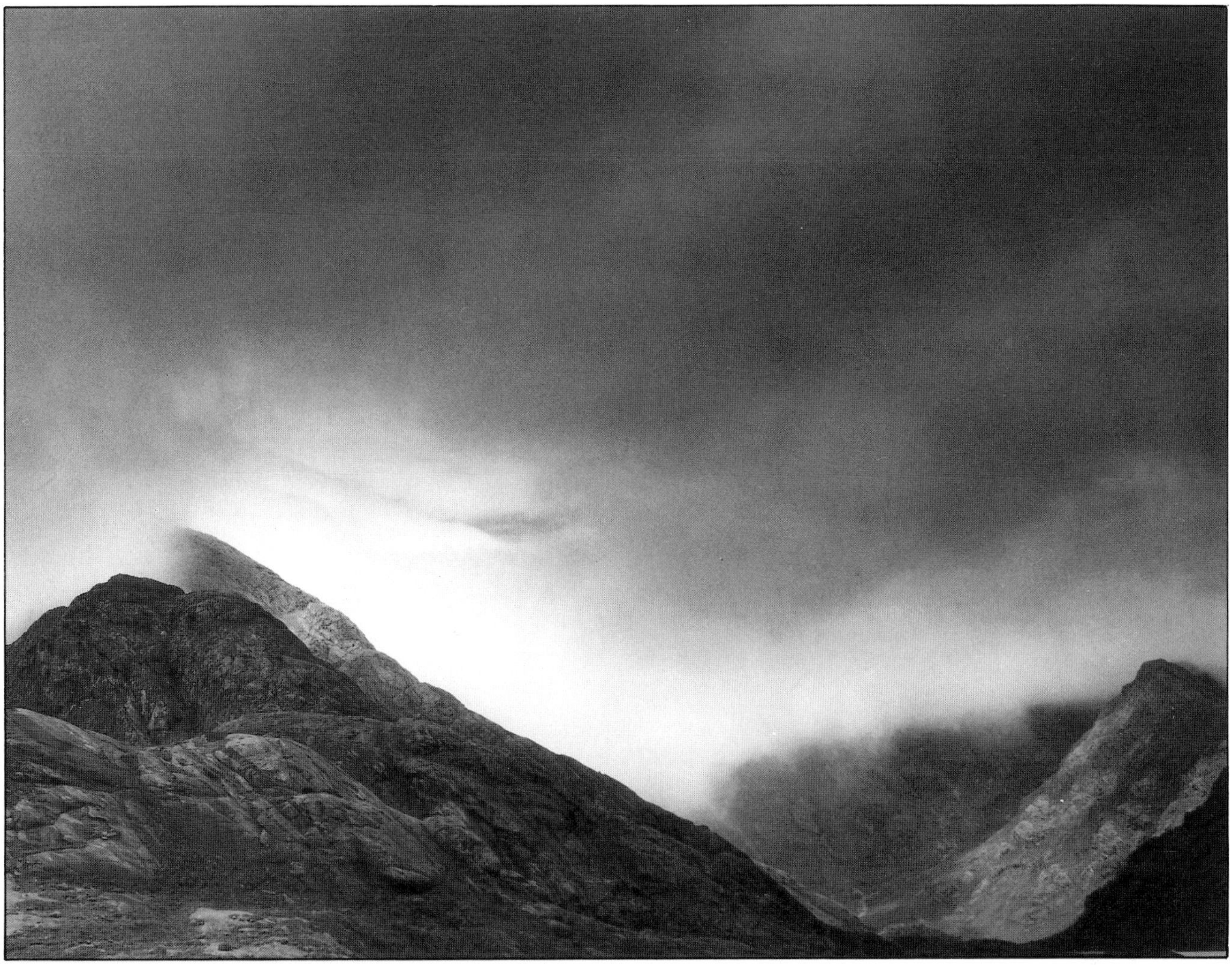

Despite their involving related techniques, blocking out and burning in produce dramatically different results, even with the same image. Burning in (above) has lightened the atmosphere of the shot, while dodging (left) has lent a sinister mood to the picture.

ABOVE Printed straight, this picture sorely lacks impact; the sky is the main culprit, being as it is bleached and devoid of detail.

RIGHT However, a simple process of burning in – selectively preventing light from reaching the print during exposure – restores sufficient contrast to the sky for the image to regain its punch.

ABOVE Burning in is more than a simple technique – it's a creative tool. And remember that you need not use specialized tools; even your hand will serve as an adequate block between the light source and the printing paper.

one of a set of differently shaped apertures cut into smaller pieces of black paper.

Some darkroom workers prefer to use their hands rather than specially-prepared tools, although this method only works for burning-in and for shading from the edge of the print inwards. You cannot successfully shade an isolated area within the image by using your hand – your wrist will shade adjacent parts also. In addition, you should be particularly careful when burning-in to avoid light catching the edges of the print. Nevertheless, using hands for printing controls has an advantage in that the shape of the edge can be formed by contorting your fingers, and this edge can be softened by finger movements (almost like kneading dough).

Finally, for an edge that is convoluted but needs to be shaded precisely, you can cut around the image made on a test print – this will give an exact match.

VIGNETTING

Although not used for the same purposes, and more of a special effect, vignetting is a technique that is practised in essentially the same way as burning-in. The idea is to isolate the image entirely within the white background of the printing paper, usually in a soft-oval frame. Its main use has been in printing portraits. The technique requires an oval (or other shape) cut in a large sheet of black card. This tool should be used about halfway between the enlarger and the print to give a soft edge, and so the size of the cut hole needs to be calculated in advance. The entire exposure is then made through the cut hole, so that no light at all reaches the print from the edges of the negative. It too needs to be moved constantly, but kept central to the print.

WORKING ON THE PRINT

Retouching is a skill that can be used both to correct faults and to introduce major changes and special effects. At its least noticeable and simplest, retouching is simply a matter of 'spotting': using dyes on the tip of a fine paintbrush to clear up dust specks on a print. Most retouching, in fact, is confined to tidying up the image and correcting mistakes, although as a matter of principle it is better to avoid the faults in the first place by handling the film carefully at all stages, from exposure to processing.

The level of skill that you need depends partly on the medium. Prints are much easier to work on than film, and black-and-white is easier than colour. If you shoot in 35mm, detailed retouching is all but impossible, because of the size of the negative. The larger the form of the image, the better. If, however, there is something that can be done to the negative, this will later be much more convenient than retouching each individual print made from the same negative.

There are four possible retouching techniques, and while it is only rarely that all need to be used together on the same image, they should be applied in the following order:

How to Re-Touch Prints

Reducing print density:
1. Pre-soak the print in water for 10 minutes to soften the emulsion and paper-base.

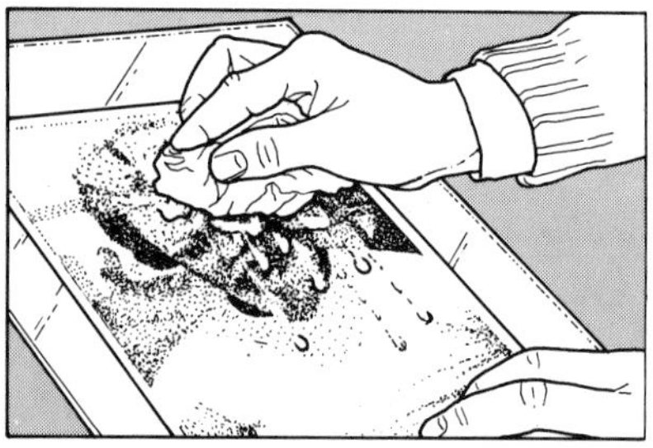

2. Lay the print on a smooth surface, such as a sheet of glass, and swab off excess water.

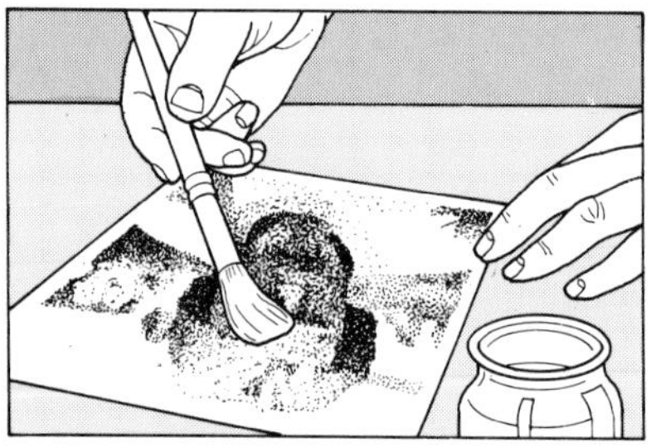

3. With brushes or cotton swabs, apply the diluted bleach or reducing solution to the print. If you are in any doubt about how fast the solution will work, or whether it will cause any discolouration, test first on an unwanted print. In any case, use a very diluted solution so that you have more control. Work the solution over the print continuously so as to avoid hard and conspicuous edges to the reduced area.

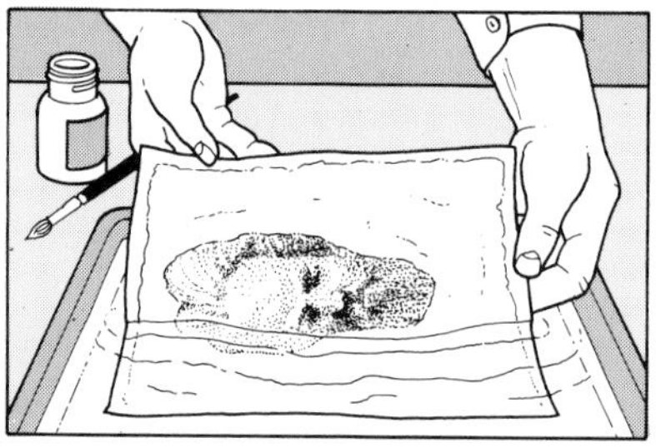

4. Use a cotton swab and either plain water or hypo to halt the bleaching action when you judge the effect to be right.

Painting with Dyes

1. Pre-soak the print in water for 10 minutes. This enables the dye to penetrate more easily, and prevents hard edges to the dye washes.
2. On a sheet of glass, or other smooth working surface, swab off water droplets and allow the print to dry slightly for about 10 minutes.
3. With either rubber cement or self-adhesive masking film, mask off the areas that are to be untreated. Using a sharp scalpel, cut round the edges of the area to be dyed with just enough pressure to break the film but not enough to damage the print. Peel off the film from the areas that have been cut round. Mix a dilute solution of dye, making sure that it matches the hue of the print. Working from two dye bottles, one brownish-black and other bluish-black, you can prepare a precise match. Apply the dye in washes with a brush. Build up the density in a number of applications. If you make a mistake, or find that the added density is too great, place the entire print under running water for several minutes and begin again.

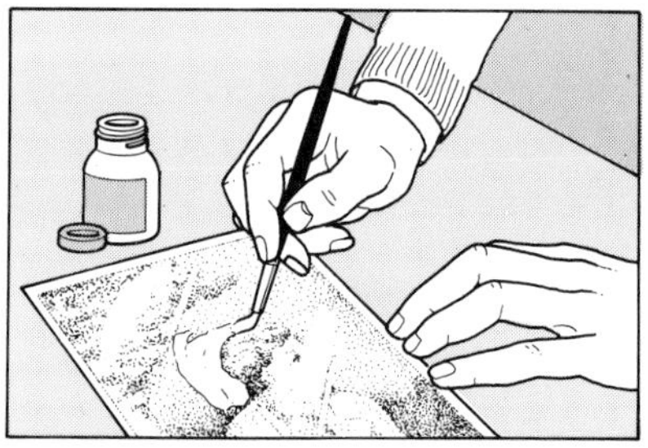

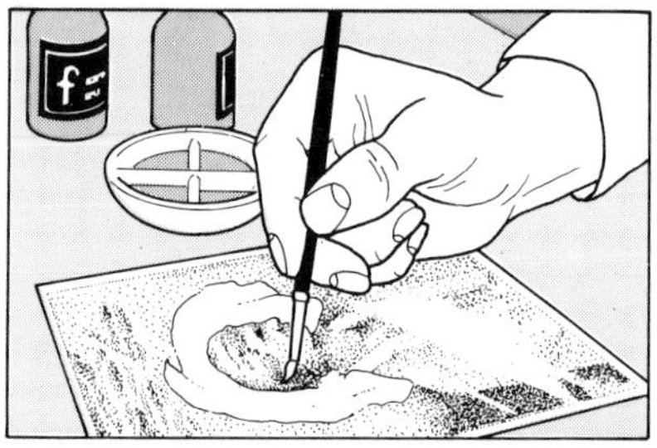

1. Chemical baths (eg reducing or intensifying the negative, or bleaching areas of the print).
2. Dyes.
3. Knifing and any other physical attention.
4. Opaque pigment.

This order is important. For instance, if you add a dye over a part of the print that has already been knifed, it will run uncontrollably into the damaged area and seep under the surrounding emulsion.

In principle, plan the retouching beforehand, starting on broad areas and finishing with the finest details. With every technique, do a little at a time, building up the effect slowly. One of the most common mistakes in retouching is to overdo it.

EQUIPMENT AND MATERIALS

For retouching a print, work on a well-lit surface: an adjustable desk-lamp is ideal. For bleaching, have a dilute solution, cotton swabs, and plenty of water available nearby to halt the bleaching effect. Sets of transparent dyes in a range of off-blacks make it possible to mix one that matches the print image exactly. Use fine camel-hair brushes, a mixing palette and water for dilution. A scalpel or razor blade is for scraping away the top layer of the print emulsion, and opaque pigments in black and white can be used (sparingly) to block out small details.

If the retouching has been so extensive that it shows in the altered surface of the print, it may be worth copying the print onto a fresh negative and then reprinting from that.

Re-Touching Equipment

Basic items are a can of compressed air (1), and an airbrush (2), with transparent masking film to cover areas not being re-touched (3). Re-touching fluid (4), gives a 'bite' to the print surface. Bleach (5) and hypo crystals (6) are also needed, and rubber cement (7) can be used for complicated masking. Watercolour pigments (8) are used in the airbrush and a scalpel (9) for cutting and knifing.

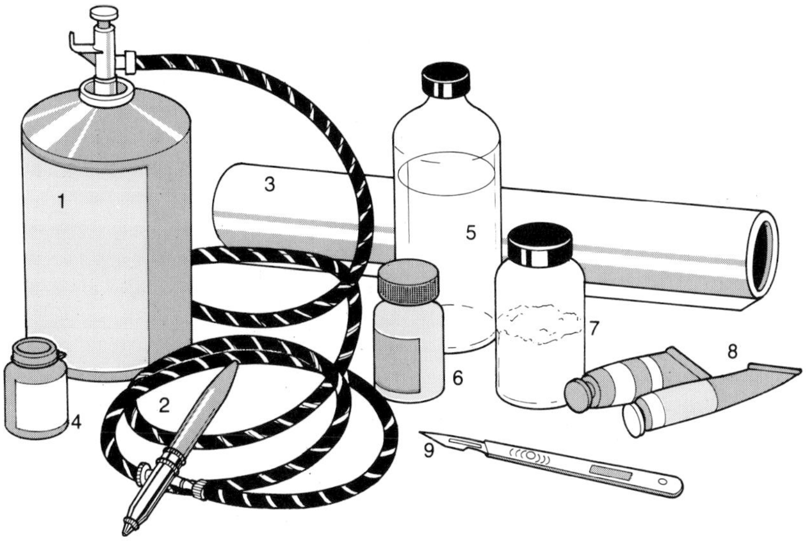

Knifing to Remove Dark Spots

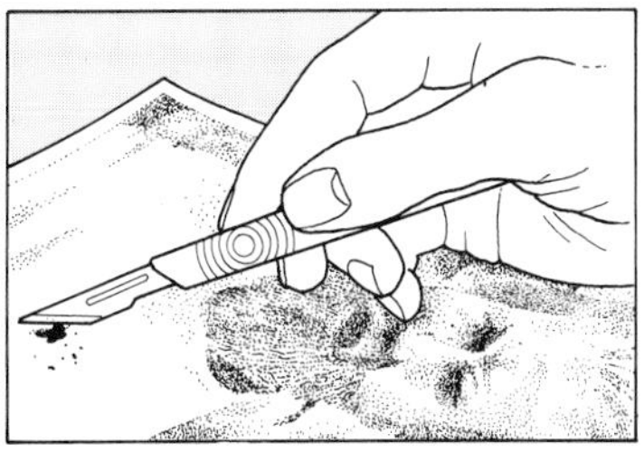

1. With the broad edge of a sharp scalpel blade, gently shave the blemish on the print's surface. Make short strokes, keeping your fingers steady and using your wrist for movement.
2. Stop before all the emulsion is removed, otherwise the roughened paper base will begin to show through.

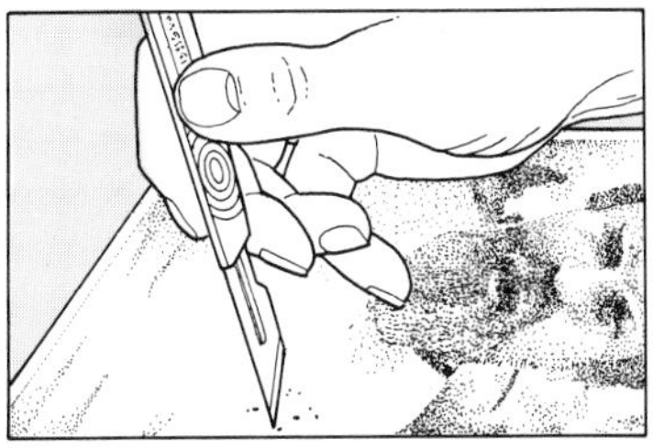

3. For small spots, use the top of the blade, but remember that there is a greater risk with this method of cutting through to the paper base. Knifing should never be done before any wet re-touching (such as bleaching or dye application) as it physically damages the print and can result in dye bleeding away from its area of application.

■ TONING

Although different makes of printing paper offer a subtle choice of colour shades in variations of black, a chemical toning solution gives a much bigger range. The most commonly used toner is sepia, but others include selenium, gold and multi-toners (which use a selection of colour couplers and a colour developer). Each has different procedures for use, and you should study the manufacturer's instructions carefully. Because toners reduce the maximum density from the original black silver, toning procedures work most successfully on prints that have been exposed and developed quite heavily.

Sepia toning, the most common method of all, is a two-part or three-part process, depending on the final effect that you are looking for. In the first stage, soak the fixed and washed print in the bleach solution provided. You can do this by inspection, for a few minutes, until the image has faded to a pale

BELOW Sepia toning remains a popular technique, giving treated prints that brownish 'aged' look.

BELOW RIGHT, TOP AND BOTTOM Compare the blue-black bias in a gold toned print (bottom) with an untreated print featuring the same image (top).

yellowish-brownish colour. Then transfer the print to the toning solution, which will restore the image in sepia. For a richer brown image, give an additional soaking in the toner for two or three minutes before the bleach bath. For different effects, it is possible, with care, to apply either the bleach or both the bleach and toner locally, using a cotton swab.

Gold toning is a single solution, one-stage process. More than most toning procedures, its effect depends heavily on the type of print emulsion and on other treatments already used. It works progressively, up to about 20min, and it takes this full time for a regular silver-bromide paper to show a change towards blue-black. Chlorobromide paper, on the other hand, turns orange-brown, while a print that has first been sepia toned will turn out purple-brown after a few minutes or orange-red if given the full soaking.

BELOW, LEFT AND RIGHT Sepia toning can be a two- or three-stage process, depending upon how strong you want the sepia effect to be. For a richer brown image (below left), give the print an additional soaking in the toner after the initial soak for another two or three minutes. As these three toned prints show, the increase in toning can be very noticeable – although it is possible to see the effect without toning a complete print. This can be done by applying locally either the bleach or bleach and toner using a cotton swab.

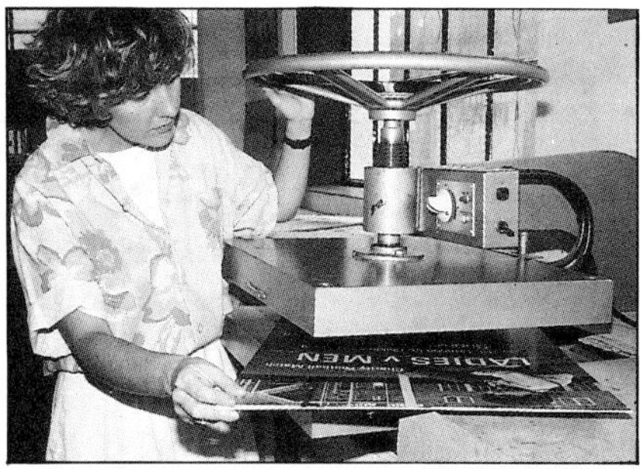

Although you can buy your own hot-mounting press, they are fairly expensive. You may wish to have your favourite prints mounted professionally.

BELOW Before investing in the materials or making an enlargement for display, decide upon how large you wish the print to appear within the frame. As can clearly be seen here, changes in size between print and frame can have a dramatic effect upon the impression the print gives.

MOUNTING PRINTS

With the final enlargement made, and spotted or retouched as necessary, you can begin to think of how to display it to best advantage. While one alternative is to leave prints loose in a box or folder, this is little protection against handling. For your best prints, consider an album or an individual mount.

In a photographic album, the paper and board should be of archival materials (some papers, and most adhesives, give off volatile compounds that will, in time, cause the image to fade and discolour). For this same reason, avoid sticking prints to paper with glue or double-sided adhesive tape. Instead, use either an album in which the pages have glassine covers that hold prints in place, or use paper corner mounts.

For a more prominent display, however, a print needs to be mounted on board. There is a special technique for this, using dry mounting tissue (this is archivally sound) and some kind of heated press. A proper press is ideal, but is also an additional expense; if you do not think its cost is justified by the number of prints you intend to mount, it is possible to make do with an ordinary household iron.

EQUIPMENT AND MATERIALS

You will need: a packet of dry mounting tissue or a photographically inert cement (Kodak, for instance, make both); mounting board, also photographically inert; a dry mounting press and tacking iron, or else a household iron set to the lowest level for a synthetic fabric; a rotary print cutter, or a sharp blade (a craft-knife or a scalpel) used with a metal straight-edge and setsquare. For

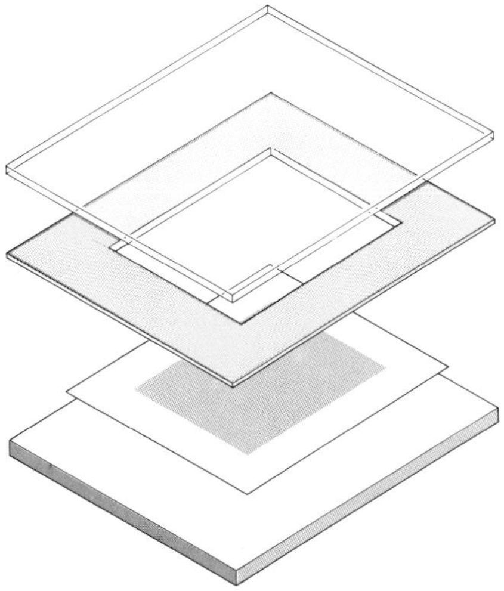

ABOVE An exploded view of the standard glass-fronted frame; avoid using glue or double-sided tape when mounting the print within the frame as this may eventually fade or discolour the print.

making overlay frames, a mat cutter is ideal, as this can be set to make an angled cut. Thin cotton gloves protect the print's surface from finger grease.

■ TRIMMING THE PRINT

This is only necessary if the print is to be displayed without an overlay frame – in other words, if the edges of the print are to remain visible. Also, if you take sufficient care in arranging the easel masks when printing, and make sure that the paper is located securely, you may not find it necessary to trim off the borders later. If you do need to trim the print, however, a rotary cutter makes the process very simple. Again, because it is an additional expense, if you expect to be making only a few prints, a blade, straightedge and setsquare will be adequate. With either a rotary blade or a craft knife, sharpen the edge regularly, or have it done professionally as necessary. Paper dulls blades very quickly.

Using a craft knife, cut over a thick piece of mounting board to protect your worktop, but move the straight-edge each time you cut to avoid running over previous incisions in the board (these can catch the blade and deflect it). Use the setsquare to ensure that the angles between the edges are at exactly 90 degrees, but cut against the metal straight-edge held next to it.

■ COLD MOUNTING

Use only an adhesive that has been made specifically for mounting photographs, or it will make the image deteriorate in time. There are no special procedures, but it is usually necessary to press the print and mounting board flat under some heavy books after the adhesive has been applied.

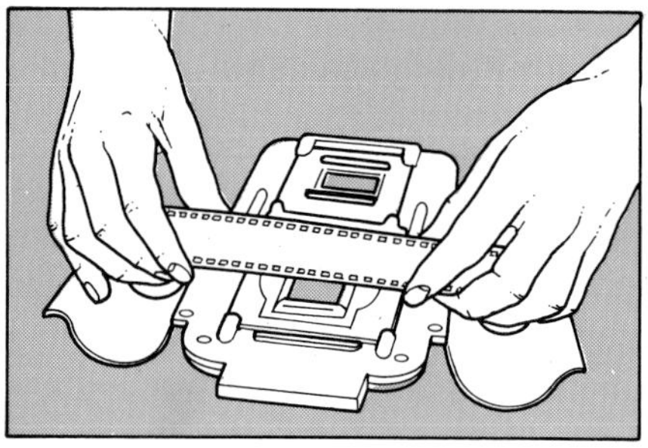

ABOVE A normal negative carrier from an enlarger accepts short strips of film, and this is the way negatives should be cut and filed.

FILING NEGATIVES

Unlike slides, which are themselves the finished product, negatives are a working stage in black-and-white photography, and need a different storage system. The images they carry do not need to be immediately easy to see, but they do need to be stored safely, and in such a way that they can be taken out and used in an enlarger rapidly. They also need a separate visual reference system – that is, accessible files of contact sheets.

A normal negative carrier in an enlarger accepts short strips of film, and this is the way negatives should be cut and filed. Avoid cutting individual frames from a roll as much as possible: a single negative is more difficult to handle, and so more likely to slip from your fingers; it will also sit less securely in most negative carriers. The usual way of cutting a roll of 36 35mm exposures is into six strips of six frames each. 6×6cm negatives from a 120 roll will normally cut into strips of three or four.

Standard negative envelopes are translucent, although transparent slips are easier for identification. In either case, the most widely used filing system is in sheets divided into sufficient strips to hold one roll of film.

Flicking through negative files in search of a particular picture is tedious and inefficient, hence the need for a full set of contact sheets. Having made the contact sheet the next step is to relate negative sheets to contact sheets, for which you will need some labelling or numbering system. One of the most straightforward methods is simply by the order in which you shot the rolls: give the same number to the negative sheet and to the contact sheet.

With a normal print, you should never write on the back in ink – the pressure of the pen may go through and emboss the emulsion, and the ink may eventually cause a stain. With a contact sheet, however, you can make an exception; use the back to write down all the essential details, such as the date, place, subject, type of film and any special procedures, such as push-processing. You might also want to include a few notes on the printing. The sheet can then be stored loose, in a box or folder, or in a ring-bound book file; negative sheets and contact sheets can be kept together or separately.

RIGHT Fortunately for the photographer, many processing labs return negatives in purpose-built folders. These are available for both 35mm (right) and 120 (far right) format films.

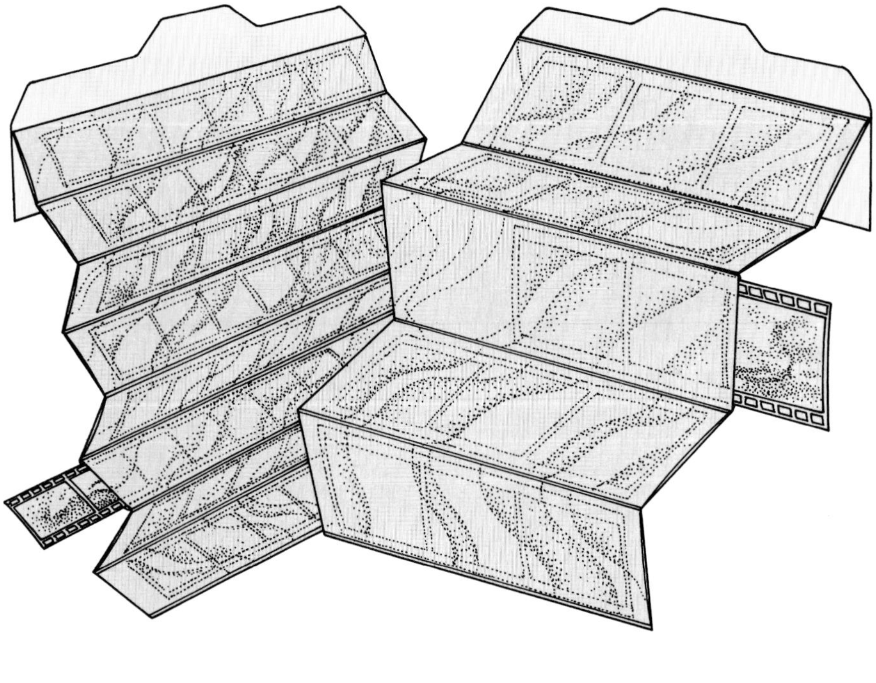

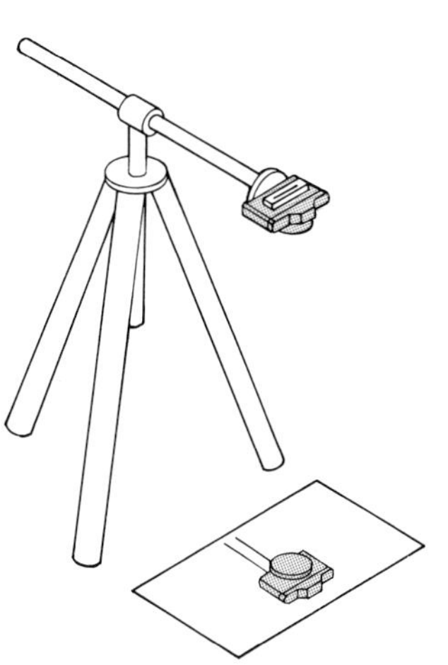

ABOVE Copying prints is a fairly simple process once a tripod fitted with a horizontal arm is employed. Ensure that the tripod legs will not appear in the picture!

COPYING NEGATIVES AND PRINTS

Making copies of important photographs is a basic skill that has several uses in caring for and restoring images. For instance, a duplicate negative can be insurance against loss or damage, or it may simply make printing easier if you enlarge it, making the dodging and burning-in corrections at this stage. Copying a print may be the only way of saving an image if the original negative has gone missing or been destroyed, and is also useful if you have already done considerable difficult retouching to a print, or have made a photo-montage by sticking parts of different prints together.

COPY NEGATIVES

The technique for copying negatives is different in principle from the slide duplicating procedures used for transparencies. Because the original is a negative, normal black-and-white emulsions are not suitable, as they produce negative images, and the result would be a transparent positive. The material needed is a direct duplicating film, and this is normally exposed in the enlarger. The normal procedure is to make the copy negative onto a large sheet of this film – large enough for contact printing later (this avoids one more optical stage). The obvious difference in exposing a sheet of direct duplicating film and a sheet of printing paper is that with the former, shorter exposures give denser images. Dodging and burning-in are possible, but the effects are reversed. The film speed is similar to that of most printing papers, and development is in a standard dish.

COPY PRINTS

This is a relatively straightforward procedure, involving normal black-and-white film. The three most important things to consider are alignment, lighting and contrast.

Alignment means getting the print absolutely straight in relation to the camera; any slight tilt of either the print or the camera will cause what is known

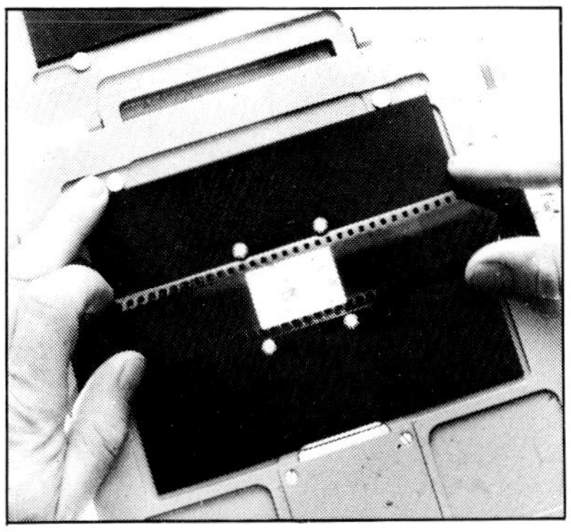

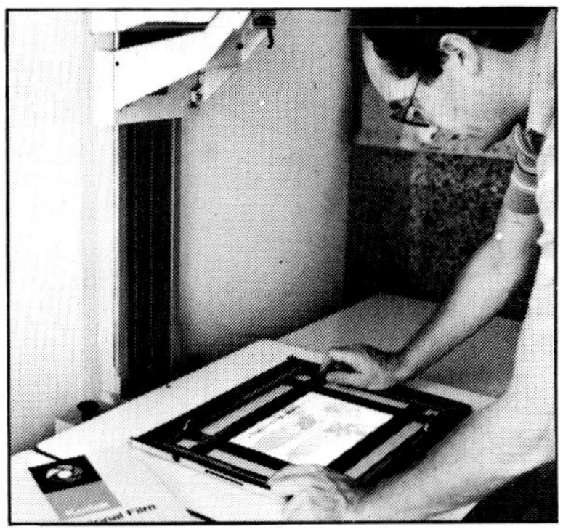

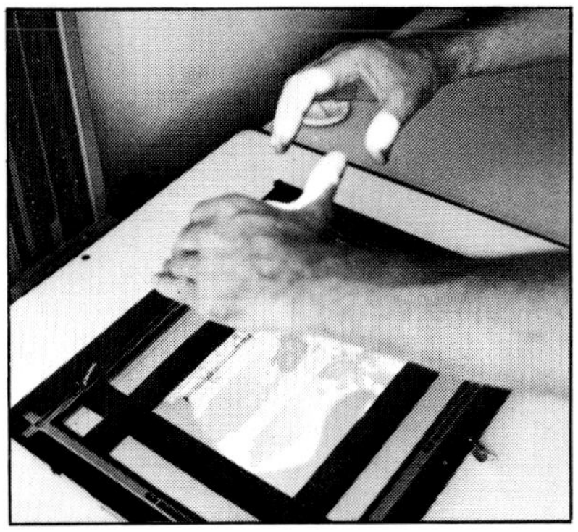

Negative Copying

1. Place the original negative in the enlarger's carrier, in exactly the same way as for printing.
2. Using a regular printing easel, focus and frame the image.
3. Using a weak red safelight (the duplicating film is sensitive only to blue light), expose the film. A test strip may be necessary to calculate the exact exposure time and aperture setting. Here, the shadowy areas are shaded to hold detail. Develop for about 2 to 2½ minutes in a dish. (The actual time will depend on the developer and on the level of contrast desired). Rinse in water for 30 seconds. Fix for 5 to 10 minutes, agitating frequently. Wash for 20 to 30 minutes in running water. After a weak bath of wetting agent, hang to dry.

ABOVE With the 50mm enlarger lens stopped down to f11 for maximum sharpness, this 35mm negative was exposed for 30 seconds and the 8 × 10 inch (20 × 24cm) copy negative developed for two minutes in Kodak D-163.

LEFT Enlarging a 35mm negative onto 8 × 10 inch (20 × 24cm) duplicating film involves a magnification of about eight times, but this is no more than is necessary for a normal print, and although the graininess becomes much more obvious, and the resolution appears to deteriorate, the final result, by contact-printing the enlarged duplicate negative, is no different from what would have been achieved by making a straightforward print enlargement.

as 'key-stoning', in which the rectangular image becomes a trapezoid with two of the sides converging. If you lay the print flat and point the camera vertically down, the easiest method of alignment is to use a two-way spirit level on both the print and the camera back. Vertical copying like this is probably the most convenient method of all, and can be done either with a purpose-built copying stand, or with a tripod (if the latter, be careful that the legs are not in the way of the lighting, or they will cast a shadow over the print). A slightly more complex, but very efficient alternative is to use your enlarger, placing an unexposed strip of film in the negative carrier and the print on the baseboard; with this technique, another negative must first be used in order to focus the enlarger at the right distance.

A second method of alignment is to place a small flat mirror on the print, in the middle. The camera lens is then re-focused and the camera angle adjusted until the reflection of the lens is centred in the viewfinder. This is extreemly accurate. Adjust the focus again before making the exposure . If your camera has the facility for interchangeable viewing screens, you might consider fitting one that has a checked grid pattern. This pattern will make it clear when the camera and print are properly aligned, although you must then leave a small distance surrounding the print in the viewfinder.

When lighting a print in order to make a copy, the two key factors are even coverage and avoiding reflections. For even lighting, arrange two lamps, at equal distance from the print and on opposite sides. To avoid a 'hot spot' in the centre, aim each lamp towards the opposite edge of the print; the two beams will cross and the light will be evenly distributed. If you have only one light, this can be used when copying a fairly small print, provided that you place a strong reflector, such as crumpled foil, on the side opposite.

As a test of lighting evenness, use a hand-held meter fitted with a plastic dome for incident readings, and measure the light level in each corner. Another, more rough-and-ready technique is to cover the print with a sheet of plain white paper, and hold a pencil vertically over the middle so that its tip is just touching: the two shadows cast should be of equal length and density.

Reflections in the print's surface are possible, particularly if the surface sheen is glossy. First make sure that the print lies flat, weighing down the corners or placing it in the enlarger easel. Then make sure that the lamps are at a sufficiently acute angle to the print – 45 degrees or less. The most certain way of blocking reflections is to support a large sheet of black card or paper just in front of the camera, with a hole cut in it just large enough for the lens.

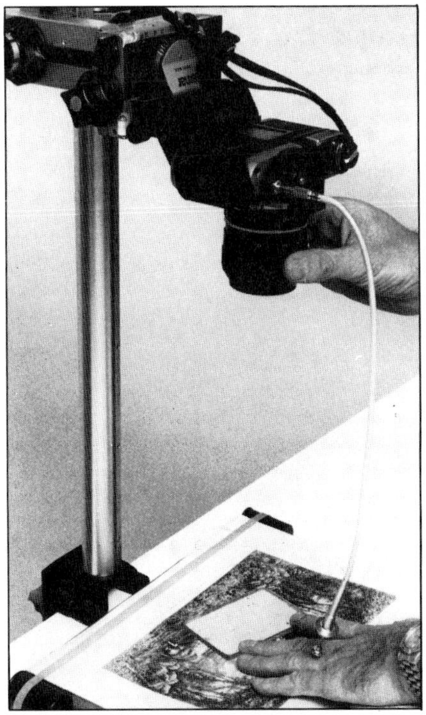

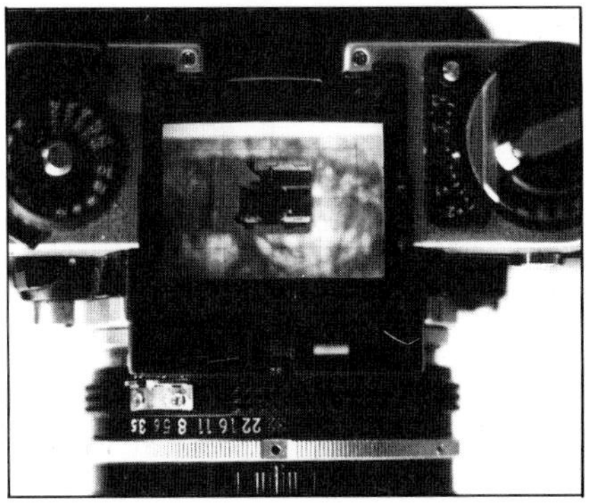

ABOVE The viewing prism can be detached from certain, top-of-the-range SLRs, and this makes the business of focusing far easier.

TOP When using your SLR on a copying stand, attach a cable release. This will prevent the camera from shaking during exposure, thus ensuring the sharpest possible results.

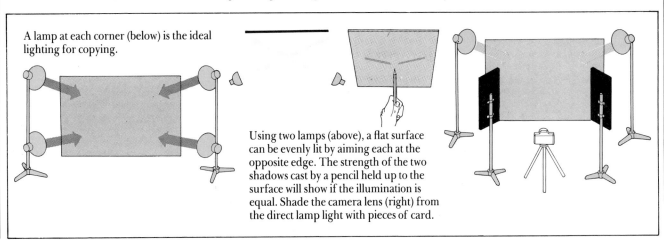

A lamp at each corner (below) is the ideal lighting for copying.

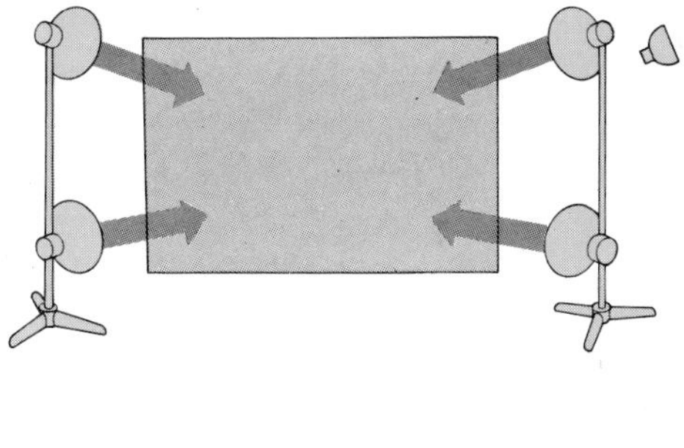

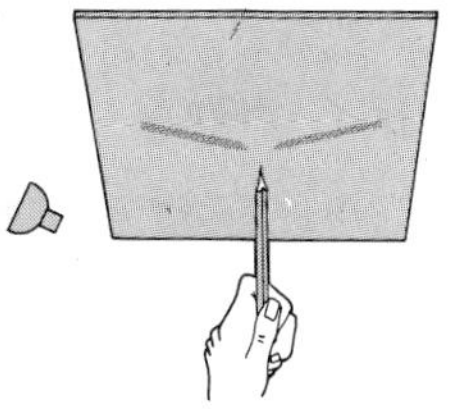

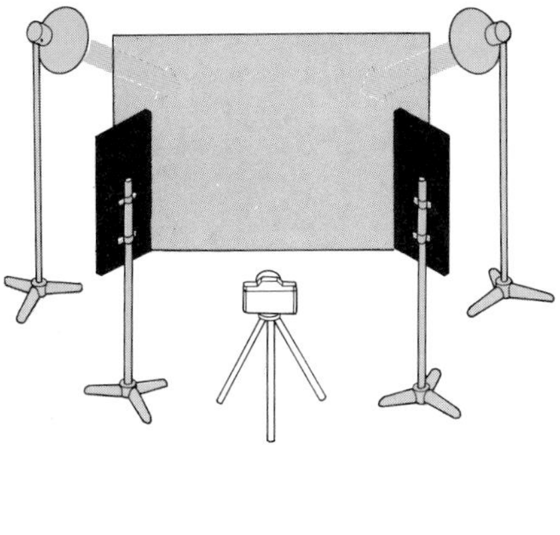

Using two lamps (above), a flat surface can be evenly lit by aiming each at the opposite edge. The strength of the two shadows cast by a pencil held up to the surface will show if the illumination is equal. Shade the camera lens (right) from the direct lamp light with pieces of card.

A

Aberration. Lens fault in which light rays are scattered, thereby degrading the image.
Aerial Perspective. The impression of depth in a scene that is conveyed by haze.
Angle of view. The widest angle of those light rays accepted by a lens that form an acceptably sharp image at the film plane. This angle is widest when the lens is focused at infinity.
Aperture. In most lenses, the aperture is an adjustable circular hole centred on the lens axis. It is the part of the lens system that admits light.
ASA. Arithmetically progressive rating of the sensitivity of a film to light (American Standards Association). ASA 200 film, for example, is twice as fast as ASA 100 film.
Automatic exposure control. Camera system where the photo-electric cell that measures the light reaching the film plane is linked to the shutter or lens aperture to adjust the exposure automatically.

B

Back lighting. Lighting from behind the subject directed towards the camera position.
Barrel distortion. A lens aberration in which the shape of the image is distorted. The magnification decreases radially outwards, so that a square object appears barrel-shaped, with the straight edges bowed outwards.
Base. The support material for an emulsion – normally plastic or paper.
Between-the-lens shutter. A leaf shutter located inside a compound lens, as close as possible to the aperture diaphragm.
Bounce flash. Diffusion of the light from a flash unit, by directing it towards a reflective surface, such as a ceiling or wall. This scatters the light rays, giving a softer illumination.
Bracketing. A method of compensating for uncertainties in exposure, by making a series of exposures of a single subject, each varying by a progressive amount from the estimated correct aperture/speed setting.

C

Camera shake. Unintentional movement of the camera during exposure, causing unsharpness in the image.
CdS cell. Cadmium sulphide cell used commonly in through-the-lens light meters. Its proportionate resistance to the quantity of light received is the basis of exposure measurement.
Characteristic curve. Curve plotted on a graph from two axes – exposure and density – used to describe the characteristics and performance of sensitive emulsions.
Circle of confusion. The disc of light formed by an imaginary lens. When small enough, it appears to the eye as a point, and at this size the image appears sharp.
Coating. A thin deposited surface on a lens, used to reduce flare.
Colour compensating filter. Filter used to alter tones. Available in primary and complementary colours at different strengths.
Colour conversion filter. Coloured filter that alters the colour temperature of light.
Colour temperature. The temperature to which an inert substance would have to be heated in order for it to glow at a particular colour. The scale of colour temperature significant for photography ranges from the reddish colours of approximately 2000°K through standard 'white' at 5400°K, to the bluish colours above 6000°K.
Complementary colours. A pair of colours that, when combined together in equal proportions, produces white light (by means of the additive process).
Compound lens. Lens constructed of more than one element, which enables various optical corrections to be made.
Condenser. Simple lens system that concentrates light into a beam.
Contact sheet. A print of all the frames of a roll of film arranged in strips, same-size, from which negatives can be selected for enlargement.
Contrast. Difference in brightness between adjacent areas of tone. In photographic emulsions, it is also the rate of increase in density measured against exposure.
Converging lens. Lens which concentrates light rays towards a common point. Also known as a convex lens.
Covering power. The diameter of useable image produced at the focal plane by a lens when focused at a given distance.

D

Definition. The subjective effect of graininess and sharpness combined.
Density. In photographic emulsions, the ability of a developed silver deposit to block transmitted light.
Depth of field. The distance through which the subject may extend and still form an acceptably sharp image, in front of and beyond the plane of critical focus. Depth of field can be increased by stopping the lens down to a smaller aperture.
Depth of focus. The distance through which the film plane can be moved and still record an acceptably sharp image.
Diaphragm. An adjustable opening that controls the amount of light passing through a lens.
Diffraction. The scattering of light waves that occurs when they strike the edge of an opaque surface.
Diffuser. Material that scatters transmitted light.
DIN. Logarithmically progressive rating of the sensitivity of a film to light (Deutsche Industrie Norm).
Diverging lens. Lens which causes light rays to spread outwards from the optical axis.

E

Electromagnetic spectrum. The range of frequencies of electromagnetic radiation, from radio waves to gamma rays, including visible radiation (light).
Electronic flash. Artificial light source produced by passing a charge across two electrodes in a gas.
Emulsion. Light-sensitive substance composed of halides suspended in gelatin, used for photographic film and paper.
Exposure. In photography, the amount of light reaching an emulsion, being the product of intensity and time.
Exposure latitude. For film, the increase in exposure that can be made from the minimum necessary to record shadow detail, while still presenting highlight detail.
Extension. A fixed or adjustable tube placed between the lens and camera body, used to increase the magnification of the image.

F

f-stop. The notation for relative aperture which is the ratio of the focal length to the diameter of the aperture. The light-gathering power of lenses is usually described by the widest f-stop they are capable of, and lens aperture rings are normally calibrated in a standard series: f1, f1.4, f2, f2.8, f4, f5.6, f8, f11, f16, f22, f32 and so on, each of these stops differing from its adjacent stop by a factor of 2.

Film speed rating. The sensitivity of a film to light, measured on a standard scale, normally either ASA or DIN.

Filter. Transparent material fitted to a lens altering the characteristics of light passing through it.

Fish-eye lens. A very wide-angle lens characterized by extreme barrel distortion.

Flare. Non-image-forming light caused by scattering and reflection, that degrades the quality of an image. Coating is often used to reduce it.

Flash. See electronic flash.

Flash guide number. Notation used to determine the aperture setting when using electronic flash unit.

Flash synchronization. Camera system that ensures that the peak light output from a flash unit coincides with the time that the shutter is fully open.

Focal length. The distance betwee the centre of a lens (the principal point) and its focal point.

Focal plane. The plane at which a lens forms a sharp image.

Focal plane shutter. Shutter located close to the focal plane, using two blinds that form an adjustable gap which moves across the film area. The size of the gap determines the exposure.

Focal point. The point on either side of a lens where light rays entering parallel to the axis converge.

Focus. The point at which light rays are converged by a lens.

G

Gelatin. Substance used to hold halide particles in suspension, in order to construct an emulsion. This is deposited on a backing.

Grade. Clarification of photographic printing paper by contrast. Grades 0 to 4 are the most common, although they are not precisely comparable across makes.

Grain. An individual light-sensitive crystal, normally of silver bromide.

Graininess. The subjective impression when viewing a photograph of granularity under normal viewing conditions. The eye cannot resolve individual grains, only overlapping clumps of grains.

Granularity. The measurement of the size and distribution of grains in an emulsion.

Ground glass screen. Sheet of glass finely ground to a translucent finish on one side, used to make image focusing easier when viewing.

Gyro stabilizer. Electrically-powered camera support that incorporates a heavy gyroscope to cushion the camera from vibrations. Particularly useful when shooting from helicopters, cars and other vehicles.

H

Hardener. Chemical agent – commonly chrome or potassium alum – that combines with the gelatin of a film to make it more resistant to scratching.

Hyperfocal distance. The minimum distance at which a lens records a subject sharply when focused at infinity.

Hypo. Alternative name for fixer, sodium thiosulphate.

Hypo eliminator. Chemical used to clear fixer from an emulsion to shorten washing time.

I

Incident light reading. Exposure measurement of the light source that illuminates the subject (of refracted light reading). It is therefore independent of the subject's own characteristics.

Infra-red radiation. Electromagnetic radiation from 730 nanometers to 1mm, longer in wavelength than light. It is emitted by hot bodies.

Intensifier. Chemical used to increase the density or contrast of an image or an emulsion. Particularly useful with too-thin negatives.

Inverse Square Law. As applied to light, the principle that the illumination of a surface by a point source of light is proportional to the square of the distance from the source to the surface.

ISO. International film speed rating system (International Standards Organisation). Arithmetic ISO speeds are effectively identical to ASA (qv) and logarithmic ISO speeds are effectively identical to DIN.

J

Joule. Unit of electronic flash output, equal to one watt-second. The power of different units can be compared with this measurement.

K

Kelvin. The standard unit of thermodynamic temperature, calculated by adding 273 to degrees centigrade.

L

Latent image. The invisible image formed by exposing an emulsion to light. Development renders it visible.

Lens. A transparent device for converging or diverging rays of light by refraction. Convex lenses are thicker at the centre than at the edges; concave lenses are thicker at the edges than at the centre.

Lens axis. A line through the centre of curvature of a lens.

Lens flare. Non-image forming light-reflected from lens surfaces that degrades the quality of the image.

Lens shade. Lens attachment that shades the front element from non-image forming light that can cause flare.

Lith film. Very high contrast film, which can be developed so that the image contains only full-density black, with no intermediate tones.

Long-focus lens. Lens with a focal length longer than the diagonal of the film format. For 35mm film, anything longer than about 50mm is therefore long-focus, although in practice the term is usually applied to lenses with at least twice the standard focal length.

Luminance. The quantity of light emitted by or reflected from a surface.

M

Masking. Blocking specific areas of an emulsion from light. For example, a weak positive image, when combined with the negative, can be used to mask the highlights so as to produce a less contrasty print.

Mirror lens. Compound lens that forms an image by reflection from curved mirrors rather than by refraction through lenses. By folding the light paths, its length is much

Robert Frank, London 1951; American Frank was the master of randomness and influenced many of today's photographers.

shorter than that of traditional lenses of the same focal length.

Monopod. Single leg of a tripod, as a light-weight and easily portable camera support for handheld shooting.

N

Negative. Photographic image with reversed tones used to make a positive image, normally a print by projection.

Neutral density. Density that is equal across all visible wavelengths.

Normal lens. Lens with a focal length equal to the diagonal of the film format. It produces an image which appears to have normal perspective and angle of view.

O

Open flash. Method of illuminating a subject with a flash unit, by leaving the camera shutter open, and triggering the flash discharge manually.

Optical axis. Line passing through the centre of a lens system. A light ray following this line would not be bent.

Orthochromatic film. Film that is sensitive to green and blue light, but reacts weakly to red light.

P

Panning. A smooth rotation of the camera so as to keep a moving subject continuously in frame.

Photo-electric cell. Light sensitive cell used to measure exposure. Some cells produce electricity when exposed to light; others react to light by offering an electrical resistance.

Photoflood. Tungsten lamp used in photography, with a colour temperature of 3400°K.

Photomacrography. Close-up photography with magnifications in the range of × 1 to × 10.

Photomicrography. Photography at great magnifications using the imaging systems of a microscope.

Polarization. Restriction of the direction of vibration of light. Normal light vibrates at right angles to its direction of travel in every plane; a plane-polarizing filter (the most common in photography) restricts this vibration to one plane only. There are serveral applications, the most usual being to eliminate reflections from water and non-metallic surfaces.

Primary colours. A set of any three colours that, when mixed together can be used to make any other colour, and when mixed together in equal proportions produce either white (by the additive process) or black (by the subtractive process). Red, green and blue are one set of primary colours; cyan, magenta and yellow are another.

Printing-in. Photographic printing technique of selectively increasing exposure over certain areas of the image.

Prism. Transparent substance shaped so as to refract light in a controlled manner.

Process lens. Flat-field lens designed to give high resolution of the image on a flat plane. This is achieved at the expense of depth of

field, which is always shallow.
Programmed shutter. Electronically operated shutter with variable speeds that is linked to the camera's TTL meter. When a particular aperture setting is selected, the shutter speed is automatically adjusted to give a standard exposure.

R

Rangefinder. Arrangement of mirror, lens and prism that measures distance by means of a binocular system. Used on direct viewfinder cameras for accurate focusing.
Reciprocity failure (reciprocity effect). At very short and very long exposure, the reciprocity law ceases to hold true, and an extra exposure is needed. Reciprocity failure differs from emulsion to emulsion.
Reciprocity Law. EXPOSURE = INTENSITY × TIME. In other words, the amount of exposure that the film receives in a camera is a product of the size of the lens aperture (intensity) and the shutter speed (time).
Reducer. Chemical used to remove silver from a developed image, so reducing density. Useful for over-exposed or over-developed negatives.
Reflected light reading. Exposure measurement of the light reflected from the subject (cf incident light reading). Through-the-lens meters use this method, and it is well-suited to subjects of average reflectance.
Reflector. Surface used to reflect light. Usually it diffuses the light at the same time.
Refraction. The bending of light rays as they pass from one transparent medium to another when the two media have different light-transmitting properties.
Resolution. The ability of a lens to distinguish between closely-spaced objects, also known as resolving power.
Reversal film. Photographic emulsion which, when developed, gives a positive image (commonly called a transparency). So called because of one stage in the development when the film is briefly re-exposed, either chemically or to light thus reversing the image which would in the normal way be negative.
Rifle stock. Camera support that enables a camera normally with a long lens, to be hand-held more securely, in the same manner as a rifle.

S

Safelight. Light source used in a darkroom with a colour and intensity that does not affect the light-sensitive materials for which it is designed.
Scoop. Smoothly curving studio background, used principally to eliminate the horizon line.
Selenium cell. Photo-electric cell which generates its own electricity in proportion to the light falling on it.
Sensitivity. The ability of an emulsion to respond to light.
Shading. Photographic printing technique where light is held back from selected parts of the image.
Short-focus lens. Lens with a focal length shorter than the diagonal of the film format. For the 35mm format, short-focus lenses generally range shorter than 35mm.
Shutter. Camera mechanism that controls the period of time that image-focusing light is allowed to fall on the film.
Single lens reflex. Camera design that allows the image focused on the film plane to be previewed. A hinged mirror that diverts the light path is the basis of the system.
Slave unit. Device that responds to the light emission from one flash unit, to activate additional flash units simultaneously.
Snoot. Generally, cylindrical fitting for a light source, used to throw a circle of light on the subject.
Soft-focus filter. A glass filter with an irregular or etched surface that reduces image sharpness and increases flare, in a controlled fashion. Normally used for flattering effect in portraiture and beauty shots.
Spot meter. Hand-held exposure meter of great accuracy, measuring reflected light over a small, precise angle of view.
Stop bath. Chemical that neutralizes the action of the developer on an emulsion, effectively stopping development.

T

Test strip. Test of various exposures made with an enlarger.
Through-the-lens (TTL) meter. Exposure meter built in to the camera, normally located close to the instant-return mirror of a single lens reflex or to the pentaprism.
Tone. Uniform density in an image.
Toner. Chemicals that add an overall colour to a processed black-and-white image, by means of bleaching and dyeing.
Tungsten-halogen lamp. Tungsten lamp of improved efficiency, in which the filament is enclosed in halogen gas, which causes the vaporized parts of the filament to be re-deposited on the filament rather than on the envelope.
Tungsten lighting. Artificial lighting caused by heating a filament of tungsten to a temperature where it emits light.

U

Ultra-violet radiation. Electromagnetic radiation from 13 to 397 nanometers, shorter in wavelength that light. Most films, unlike the human eye, are sensitive to ultra-violent radiation.

V

Vapour discharge lighting. Artificial lighting produced by passing an electric current through gas at low pressure in a glass envelope.
Variable contrast paper. Printing paper with a single emulsion which can be used at different degrees of contrast by means of selected filters.

W

Wetting agent. Chemical that weakens the surface tension of water, and so reduces the risk of drying marks on film.
Wide-angle lens. Lens with an angle of view wider than that considered subjectively normal by the human eye (ie more than about 50°). Wide angles of view are characteristic of lenses with short focal lengths.

Z

Zone System. A method of evaluating exposure, with implications for the photographic approach to a subject, developed by Ansel Adams, Minor White and others. Light measurement is converted to exposure settings by dividing the tonal range into specific numbered zones.
Zoom lens. Lens with a continuously variable focal length over a certain range at any given focus and aperture. It is generated by differential movement of the lens elements.

Page references to captions are given in *italic*.

PICTURE CREDITS AND ACKNOWLEDGMENTS

The author and publishers would like to thank the following for providing information and equipment for photography:

Durst Phototechnik; Jessop of Leicester Ltd., Minolta (UK) Ltd; Mosta Posta, London; Olympus Optical Co. Ltd.; Pentax (UK) Ltd.; Polaroid (UK) Ltd.

Special thanks are also due to Mark Payton.

All photographs taken by Michael Freeman, with the exception of the following:

Peter Conrad (Space Frontiers) p6; Gustave le Gray (Victoria and Albert Museum) p7; André Kertesz p8; E.T. Archive p9 (below); David Kilpatrick pp 29, 68 (right), 71 74 (left), 91; Robert Frank p154.